Kristi Coulter

Nothing Good Can Come from This

Kristi Coulter holds an M.F.A. in creative writing from the University of Michigan. She is a former Ragdale resident and the recipient of a grant from the National Foundation for Advancement in the Arts. Her work has appeared in *The Awl*, *Marie Claire*, *Vox*, *Quartz*, and other publications. She lives in Seattle.

Nothing Good
Can Come from This

Nothing Good
Can Come from This

ESSAYS

Kristi Coulter

MCD x FSG Originals

Farrar, Straus and Giroux

New York

MCD × FSG Originals
Farrar, Straus and Giroux
175 Varick Street, New York 10014

Library of Congress Cataloging-in-Publication Data
Names: Coulter, Kristi, 1970– author.
Title: Nothing good can come from this : essays / Kristi Coulter.
Description: First edition. | New York : MCD / FSG Originals, 2018.
Identifiers: LCCN 2017038355 | ISBN 9780374286200 (softcover) |
    ISBN 9780374717087 (ebook)
Classification: LCC PS3603.O88635 A6 2018 | DDC 814/.6—dc23
LC record available at https://lccn.loc.gov/2017038355

Designed by Jonathan D. Lippincott

Our books may be purchased in bulk for promotional, educational,
or business use. Please contact your local bookseller or the Macmillan
Corporate and Premium Sales Department at 1-800-221-7945, extension
5442, or by e-mail at MacmillanSpecialMarkets@macmillan.com.

www.fsgoriginals.com • www.fsgbooks.com
Follow us on Twitter, Facebook, and Instagram at @fsgoriginals

1   3   5   7   9   10   8   6   4   2

For John

Look me in the eye, then tell me that I'm satisfied.
                                          —Paul Westerberg

Contents

Nothing Good Can Come from This

Debrief

You've just described a hole to me.
Yes.

And you've made attempts to fill that hole, yes?
Yes.

How did you try to fill the hole?
I told you, wine.

Anything else?
Champagne. Cocktails. Scotch.

Beer?
Not beer.

Anything else?
Acupuncture, amino acids, applause, burning letters, cigarettes, cocks, cuffs, Ecstasy, forgiveness, fury, glutamine,
gospel choirs, gratitude, hypnosis, kava, kirtan, lipstick,

lucid dreaming, Prada, psychics, punk rock, Reiki, smudging, straight As, sweat, tarot, tongues, vortexes, yoga, zazen.

But mostly wine.

And did you fill the hole?
No. Turns out there wasn't a hole after all. Just a space.

A space.
Yes.

And have you filled the space?
Not yet.

Enjoli

I'm newly sober and dog-paddling through the booze all around me. At first I tried to avoid it by skipping parties and happy hours and dinners out. But even a social recluse has to buy food and go to work, and it turns out those are now danger zones, too. It's summer, and Whole Foods has planted rosé throughout the store. Rosé is great with fish! And strawberries! And vegan protein powder! (Okay, I made that last one up.) At the office, every desk near mine has a bottle of wine or liquor on it in case people are too lazy to walk fifty feet to one of the well-stocked communal bars we've built on our floor. Driving home from work, I pass billboard ads for Fluffed Marshmallow Smirnoff and Iced Cake Smirnoff and not just Cinnamon but Cinnamon *Churros* Smirnoff. A local pharmacy, the same one that fucked up my prescription three months in a row, installed self-service beer taps, and young men line up with their empty growlers all the way back to Eye & Ear Care.

At work, I'm co-teaching an executive leadership course. To capture their full attention, we sequester the participants at luxury retreat centers, confining them to conference rooms all day and sometimes into the night. People get so stir-crazy that the late-night bar scene has become legendary; the executives who spent all day focused on measuring their dicks end up singing karaoke and hugging. I've begged off all week. I know it makes me look standoffish, but faking enjoyment in a roomful of drunk alpha males is more than I'm ready for. Which is fine until the mandatory company-sponsored wine tasting. My plan was to work the room with my soda and lime, making sure I was seen and then leaving before things got sloppy (which they always do). Six different wines and four beers are on display at the catering stand, but when I ask for club soda, I get a blank look. Just water, then. The bartender grimaces apologetically. "I think there's a water fountain in the lobby?"

There is. But it's broken. I mingle empty-handed for fifteen minutes, fending off well-meaning offers to get me something from the bar. After the fifth, I realize I'm going to cry if one more person offers me alcohol. I leave and cry anyway. Later I order vanilla ice cream from room service to cheer myself up, and the guy says, "People love this with a shot of bourbon poured over it—want to treat yourself?"

This is the summer I realize that everyone around me is tanked. It also dawns on me that the women are *super-double* tanked. I try to find refuge at an afternoon showing of *Magic Mike*, where a group of women are drinking champagne through straws and toasting their ability to claim their Girl Time. "We've *earned* this!" they crow. There's a baby shower in progress at the nail salon. Except for the guest of honor, everyone is drinking wine, lots of it. "Thank God there are places like this where we can have lady time," a woman in a yellow dress says. "I'm going to feel hungover by dinner," a different woman says. "But it's so worth it. How often do you get a chance to get away from your kids for an afternoon?" The default setting for any meetup is "drinks," meaning bar drinks. It occurs to me that I could counter-propose coffee or tea or ham sand- wiches or a walk, but just anticipating the questions—or careful lack of questions—that would follow saps what energy I haven't already spent on just getting through the day. Like almost all the women in my life, after all, I'm a drinker. Saying "How about we grab a smoothie instead?" will be as noticeable as showing up with an enormous crucifix around my neck. *How did you not see this before?* I wonder. *You were too hammered*, I answer back. That sum- mer, though, I see. Booze is the oil in our motors, the thing that keeps us purring when we should be making other kinds of noise.

One day that summer I'm wearing unwise (but cute, so cute) shoes and trip at the farmers' market, cracking my phone, blood-staining the knees of my favorite jeans, and scraping both my palms. Naturally, I post about it on Face- book as soon as I've dusted myself off. Three women who don't know I'm sober comment quickly:

"Wine. Immediately."

"Do they sell wine there?"

"Definitely wine. And maybe new shoes."

Have I mentioned that it's morning when this happens?

On a weekday? This isn't one of those *nightclub* farmers' markets. And the women aren't the kinds of beleaguered, downtrodden creatures you imagine drinking to get through the day. They're pretty cool chicks, the kind people ridicule for having First World Problems. Why do *they* need to drink?

Because cool chicks are still women. And there's no easy way to be a woman, because there's no *acceptable* way to be a woman. And if there's no acceptable way to be the thing you are, then maybe you drink a little. Or a lot.

The year before I get sober, I'm asked to be The Woman on a panel at the company where I work. (That was literally the pitch: "We need a woman.") Three guys and me, talking to summer interns about company culture. There are two female interns in the audience, and when it's time for questions, one says, "I've heard this can be a tough place for women to succeed. Can you talk about what it's been like for you?"

As The Woman, I assume the question is directed at me. "If you're tough and persistent and thick-skinned, you'll find your way," I say. "I have."

I don't mention how she'll have to work around interruptions and invisibility and micro-aggressions and a scarcity of role models and a lifetime of her own conditioning. My job on this panel is to make this place sound good, so I leave some stuff out. Particularly the fact that I'm drinking at least one bottle of wine a night to dissolve the day off me.

But she's a woman. She probably learned to read be-

tween the lines before she could read the lines themselves. She thanks me and sits down.

"I disagree," says the guy sitting next to me. "I think
this is a great company for women."

My jaw falls open.

The guy next to him nods. "Absolutely," he says. "I have
two women on my team, and they get along great with
everyone."

Of course they do, I think. *It's called camouflage.*

Guy No. 1 continues. "There's a woman on my team
who had a baby last year. She went on maternity leave and
came back, and she's doing fine. We're very supportive of
moms."

Guy No. 3 jumps in just to make sure we have
100 percent male coverage on the topic. "The thing about
this place," he says, "is it's a meritocracy. And merit is gen-
der blind." He smiles at me and I stare back. Silent bale-
fulness is all I have to offer, but his smile wavers, so I know
I've pierced some level of smug.

The panel organizer and I fume afterward. "Those fucking fucks," she says. *"Ratfucks."*

What's a girl to do when a bunch of dudes have just told
her, in front of an audience, that she's wrong about what
it's like to be *herself*? I could talk to them, one by one, and
tell them how it felt. I could tell the panel organizer, *This
is why you never have just one of us up there.* I could make myself a superhero costume and devote the rest of my life to
vengeance on mansplainers everywhere.

Instead, I round up some girlfriends and we spend three
hours in a hipster bar, drinking rye Manhattans and eating

tapas and talking about the latest crappy, non-gender-blind things that have happened to us in meetings and on business trips and at performance review time. They toast me for taking one for the team. When we are good and numb, we Uber home, thinking, *Look at how far we've come! Level grinding our way to bigger jobs. Having first babies at forty-two, when we finally feel secure enough to take maternity leave. Planning dream vacations with the same military precision we use on the job, and feeling proud for only checking work e-mail twice a day while we're on them. We are tough enough to put up with being ignored and interrupted and underestimated every day, and smart enough to laugh it off together. We've made it. This is the good life.*

Do you remember the Enjoli perfume commercial from the 1970s? The chick who could bring home the bacon, fry it up in a pan, and never let you forget you're a man?

I blame that bitch for a lot. For spreading the notion that women should have a career, keep house, *and* fuck their husbands, when the only sane thing to do is pick two and outsource the third. For making it seem glamorous. For suggesting it was going to be *fun*. And for the tagline she dragged around: "The 8-Hour Perfume for the 24-Hour Woman." Just in case you thought you could get *one* fucking hour off the clock.

Is it really that hard, being a First World woman? Is it really so tough to have the career and the spouse and the pets and the herb garden and the core strengthening and the oh-I-just-woke-up-like-this makeup and the face injections and the Uber driver who might be a rapist? Is it so hard to work ten hours for your rightful 77 percent of a salary, walk home past a drunk who invites you to suck his cock, and turn on the TV to hear the men who run this country talk about protecting you from abortion regret by forcing you to grow children inside your body? I mean, what's the big deal? Why would anyone want to soften the edges of this glorious reality?

All summer, as I venture back out into the world, I find alcohol in places where I thought I'd be safe from it. My neighborhood yoga studio starts a monthly "Vinyasa & Vino" event—because wine is exactly what you need after an hour in a sweatbox. A local kitchen shop offers a knife-skills and wine-tasting class—yes, alcohol for people who have *already self-identified* as being so clumsy with sharp objects that they need professional instruction. I run a women's half marathon on a day when temperatures are fifteen degrees above normal. It's my second half marathon in a month (no addictive tendencies here), and with every footfall my legs feel like they're being jammed into my hip sockets. My headphones die midway, followed shortly after by my phone, so I can neither distract myself nor track my progress. It's a horror show. But I *finish*, so I get that finisher's medal, and I'm soaked, chafed, limping, but triumphant. Then someone says, "Congratulations, the margarita tent is right over there!"

One beautiful day I'm at a farm outside Seattle, petting a baby goat while another baby goat repeatedly gooses me and then bounds away. *This is fun*, I think idly, and then, less idly, *I am having a good time.* I'm not yet sixty days sober and have been focusing on just getting the basics down: how to watch Netflix without bringing a glass to my lips every minute, how to attend a work happy hour without crying. I haven't even been looking for *fun.* But it tracked me down anyway.

I sit on a picnic table and try to imagine what this would have been like a year ago. I wouldn't have been drinking *while* petting baby goats (though I bet people would pay good money to do that). But I would be either recovering from drinking the night before—and using the goats as proof that I still had other interests—or preparing for the night of drinking ahead, and hoping the goats would some-how preload enough wholesomeness or good feeling in me to help me hold back, for once. Either way, those baby animals would have been a means to an end I couldn't reach.

In the days following, I start to notice how actual experience and my expectations of it dance and conflict and how the real thing is . . . hard to sum up. Nothing in life is all one way. I laugh my ass off three times during a movie that otherwise has me checking my watch. I have sex when I don't really feel like it, thinking maybe I'll get interested midway, but I'd still rather be reading. I run a hilly route dreading how my lungs and quads will hurt, and they do, but not as much as I'd decided they would. It's maddening how subtle life is. And it's frustrating how much I want to engineer it into drama. There is nothing so absorbing or high stakes or pleasurable that I won't try to alter my natu-ral response to it. Only it's hard to do that without wine, and I'm too tired to find another route. So I trudge along doing things that are a little bit boring and a little bit fun and a little bit beautiful until my sense of scale starts to match reality.

As my expectations of life become life-sized, I lose patience with being a twenty-four-hour woman. The stranger who tells me to smile. The janitor who stares at my legs. The men on TV who want to annex my uterus. Even the other TV men who say that abortion should be "safe, legal, and rare." *What the fuck business is it of yours whether it's* rare *or not?* I think.

The magazines telling me strong is the new sexy and smart is the new beautiful, as if strong and smart are just paths to hot. The Facebook memes: muscles are beautiful. No, wait: fat is beautiful. No, wait: thin is beautiful, too, as long as you don't work for it. No, wait: *All women are beautiful!* As if we are toddlers who must be given *exactly equal* shares of princess dust or we'll lose our shit.

And then I start to get angry at women, too. Note: newly sober people can be the *teeniest* bit judgmental, especially if they were judgy to begin with, which I was. I'm burning with clarity, and I want all of womankind to burn with me so we can incinerate the patriarchy just by existing. I don't want women to blur the edges of their bad days or use wine to talk themselves down from causing righteous trouble.

Later, I'll laugh (and cringe a little) at my own zeal during this time. I'll understand that no one can be enraged 24-7 and that even sober I have my own ways of blurring the edges, not all of them great ideas. It will have dawned on me that there are women in the world who can have a glass of wine without craving the whole bottle. That some women even leave wine in the glass, a concept as alien to me as eating half an Oreo.

But the kernel of that anger still lives, and some of it is for myself. When I was drinking, I would read news articles about the impact of alcohol on female bodies, and instead of contemplating what it meant for my own cancer or heart disease risk, I'd think, *Just another scare tactic.* If I saw a story about a blind-drunk woman being raped at a frat party, I'd think, *Blaming the victim.* If I read warnings about alcohol being a depressant, I'd think, *Like real life isn't a depressant, too?*

But multiple things can be true at once. The things women enjoy *are* demonized. And women also metabolize alcohol differently than men. We *are* blamed for our own rapes. And it's also harder to sniff out danger when you're drunk. Real life *is* hard. And it's *not* fair. I didn't want to see any of this. I told myself that any bad press for drinking was just one more ploy to keep women looking over their shoulders, because if I really took it in, I'd have to ask why I was willingly destroying myself.

But who said anything about *fairness?* This isn't about what's fair. It's about what we can afford. And we can't afford this. We can't afford to live lives we have to fool our own central nervous systems into tolerating. We can't afford to be twenty-four-hour women. Trying to be one shattered me.

I slosh around in my anger for months, trudging through my first sober Christmas and job change and birthday and eventually learning to use the anger as a reminder to pay attention and go slow and choose things I actually want to happen. By the time summer comes back around, I realize I no longer smell like eight-hour perfume. I'm becoming a twenty-four-hour *person*, not a twenty-four-hour woman. And twenty-four-hour people get a lot more room to breathe.

That second summer, I meet my friend Mindy outside San Diego, where her adopted son is days from being born. Mindy's dark alleys were different from mine, but she walked them all the same and walked herself out of them, too. Sometimes, talking about the recent past, we blink at each other like people struggling to readjust to sunlight after a long, bad movie. More and more, it's the new that gets our attention: my new job, her newish and happy marriage, the book I'm writing, and the classes she's taking. The things we are making happen, step by step.

We spend the weekend moving slowly and sleeping late and wishing the lazy baby would hurry up already. On Sunday morning we're reading by the deep end of the hotel pool when the shallow end starts to fill with women—a bridal party from what we can make out. They arrive already tipsy, and the pomegranate mimosas—"pomegranate is a superfood!" one woman repeatedly tells the others—keep coming until that end of the pool seems like a Greek chorus of women with major grievances about their bodies, faces, children, homes, jobs, and husbands, who aren't going to do anything about any of it but get loaded and sunburned.

I give Mindy the look that women use to say *Do you*

believe this shit? The woman on the other side of her catches the look and gives it back to me over her laptop, and then the woman next to *her* joins in, too. We engage in a silent four-way exchange of dismay, irritation, and bitchiness, and it is wonderful.

Then Mindy slides her Tom Ford sunglasses back over her eyes and says, "All I can say is, it's really nice on this end of the pool." I laugh and my heart swells against my swimsuit and I pull my shades down, too, to keep my suddenly watery eyes to myself. Because it is. It is so nice on this end of the pool, where the book I'm reading is a letdown and my legs look too white and the ice has long since melted in my glass and work is hard and there's still no good way to be a girl and I don't know what to do with my life and I have to actually deal with all of that. Sober. I never expected to make it to this end of the pool. I never thought I'd get to be here.

Mammal, Fish, or Bird

I was running the Bluff Trail at Ebey's Landing, a historic reserve on Whidbey Island, just to the upper left of Seattle. It's named after someone named Ebey, who . . . landed there at some point, I guess. In a boat. Look, I don't know what the deal was and I don't really care. I don't know if he *earned* having his own landing, or if he just called dibs. I could probably look it up, but then so could you. I am assuming Ebey was a man, though. Women get named after nature, but it's rarely named after us.

Anyway. I was running at Ebey's Landing last September. It's a six-mile trail that starts at an old cemetery and winds past acres of beet greens; I don't know much about history, but I do know my plants, especially when they are labeled with three-foot signs that say BEETS. Past the beets, you hang a left and pass through a prairie so many shades of green it could almost make you believe in elves, and luck, and Ireland. At the end of the prairie, you climb an infuriatingly steep but short path to the bluffs, at which point you can gasp for breath while gazing at two of Washington

State's thirty-seven major mountain ranges. Then the Bluff Trail carries you for two miles high above Puget Sound and down a bunch of switchbacks to the beach, where you loop two miles back to the prairie, dreams of Ireland, beets, tombstones, and your car.

At least this is how it would go if you understood tides.

I don't understand tides. I mean, I haven't tried to. I know they have something to do with the moon, which frankly sounds a little Wiccan to me, but that doesn't mean it isn't true. The idea that my body automatically makes food for a fetus (like baking a cake just in case someone special drops by) and then gets rid of it through a hole every month doesn't sound totally legit, either, but it happens.

So, I don't get tides. And until that day at Ebey's Landing, I also did not fully grasp that they applied to me. Which is why I came trotting down the switchbacks, feeling like a world-class outdoorswoman, to find myself staring at ankle-deep water. I had two choices: continue on as planned, slogging two miles through water that, for all I knew, could be *ten feet high* within an hour, or go all the way back up that hill—the first half of it sand—and return the way I'd come.

I looked at the water. I looked up at the bluffs. "The way the planet works is totally unfair," I muttered as I started my ascent.

According to family lore, when I was three years old, my parents took me to a psychiatrist to find out why I talked so much. The dramatic high point of the testing process came during a word-association exercise that went something like this:

DOCTOR: Peanut butter.
ME: Jelly.
DOCTOR: Shoes.
ME: Socks.
DOCTOR: Nail.
ME: What?
DOCTOR: Nail.
ME: Which kind?
DOCTOR: What do you mean?
ME: I mean is it the kind on your finger, the kind on your toe, or the kind you hit with a hammer?
DOCTOR (*pauses, rises, says in stentorian tones*): This child is not mentally ill. This child is a *genius*.

Henceforth my parents saw that nothing was wrong with me, and my childhood continued in a stable, accepting environment. Ha! That totally didn't happen. Instead, I continued to act as family scapegoat for many years. But the doctor's pronouncement ensured that I was seen as smart, which gave me *something* acceptable to be, and when I started the Gifted program at school, it opened doors to a world of steadier adults and special privileges. Unfortunately, being gifted ruined me for fact-based, practical learning, like what makes boats float or how to divide one number into another. In Gifted, we wrote short stories, worked out logic problems, and played educational games like Propaganda, where we had to identify the rhetorical flaws in various claims. "Tommy came over to my house last week, and afterward our dishwasher broke down. He'd better not come over again, or the refrigerator will break!" the teacher read, and in unison a bunch of eight-year-olds would respond, "Post hoc!" We played Oregon Trail and died of dysentery. We staged a production of *Macbeth* from a kid-level script, because all kids should learn about assassination and paranoid insanity.

By contrast, the long division and state capitals taught in my regular classroom were so boring, so pedantic. (Anything I didn't want to do back then was pedantic.) I developed the notion that I was too smart to need to *know* anything. Why memorize a bunch of facts when I could problem solve on the fly or look up the answer in a *World Book Encyclopedia*? I preferred to spend my time on things that came easily, like reading and writing, because accomplishments and prizes were routes to approval in my family and I could rack those up more easily via essay contests than science fairs. Or T-ball tournaments. Or dance recitals.

I got through high school, became a National Merit Scholar, and got a free ride to college with a brain crammed with Flannery O'Connor, simplified existentialism, and a few beginning sex tips, but virtually no knowledge of the physical world beyond how to recognize maybe 5 percent of the fish I saw snorkeling. (And kids, whatever your teachers may tell you, knowing how to give a good blow job is *way* more useful than being able to point underwater and say, "Look, a tetra.")

I made it through just fine. I finished college and got a

free ride to grad school with a knowledge base consisting of French feminism, Virginia Woolf, and the word "ontological." They accepted me without my knowing how to use a compass or a tire iron and despite my belief that a solar eclipse is when the sun passes between the earth and the moon.

I headed off to Michigan with zero experience with nontropical climates, but because I had recently read *The Solace of Open Spaces*, about a frozen-solid winter on a Wyoming cattle ranch, I assumed life in Ann Arbor would be pretty much the same. I moved with pac boots, a parka rated for fifty below zero, and a ski mask that left only my eyes exposed. Once I arrived, I realized I wouldn't need a rope to navigate from my car to the door of my apartment and my cows were not at risk of crystallizing. Chastened, I enrolled in Physics for Poets as an elective but dropped it when it proved to involve actual physics.

And everything was still just fine. Turns out you don't need to know much about atoms or entropy to be considered a credible adult. Eventually, I got married and my husband, John, amused himself by inventing a game called Mammal, Fish, or Bird? in which he would name an animal and I would categorize it.

JOHN: Duck.
ME: That's a hard one.
JOHN: Is it?
ME: Well, it spends most of its time in the water, which makes it seem *sort of* like a fish. But I know it's not a fish.

JOHN: Do you? Do you know it's not a fish?
ME: I think *technically* it's a bird, but in spirit it's really more like a mammal.
JOHN: And why is that?
ME: Because it makes eye contact. I've totally made eye contact with ducks.
JOHN: I am sure you have.

I did make some progress in my war against facts. I had started running, and while it's true that running is an instinctual thing that humans have been doing since the Stone Age (or whatever the earliest age is), it's also true that it's a lot easier and less dangerous when you have some idea of what you are doing. Of course I didn't realize that until I went for my first run at age forty-two. I had been traveling heavily for work and was in need of a portable way to burn off the anger built up by all the 6:00 a.m. layovers, long TSA lines, and grim meetings.

I approached running the same way I approach anything new: by assuming I could throw myself into the thick of it and survive on wiles and charm. I put on shorts, a tank top, and some old gym shoes, went to a popular neighborhood trail, and *hauled ass* for about forty seconds before hitting a wall of hypoxia-induced nausea. I leaned over my legs until I got my breath back, then did it again. Five times in all, never more than thirty seconds at a stretch. (I was probably running about an eight-minute mile, which isn't a big deal for your average marathon-trained Kenyan but is absurd for someone who lives at sea level and hasn't moved faster than a brisk walk in decades.)

It was a painful, humiliating experience that I wanted to repeat, if only to prove I could master it. I'd go to Green Lake Park a few times a week and stagger around as if I were being chased by a blood-drenched clown. One day I wandered into a running store, and a shockingly tall red-headed teenager looked at my deplorable feet, watched me jog on a treadmill, and fitted me with a pair of shoes designed to correct my over-pronation. I hadn't known that was a condition, and it certainly never occurred to me that a shoe could be used to *fix* anything, because I tended to gravitate toward shoes that made my feet feel terrible. *This will change everything*, I thought. Well, no. But it did open me up to the idea that running was something other people had done and that there was a body of knowledge attached to it, some of which might be relevant to me.

At the bookstore one day, I saw two whole shelves devoted to running. I pulled out one of the thicker volumes and opened it at random. Well, blow me down. I had started to wonder if maybe I had only one working lung, but it turns out that there was an entire chapter on breathing. I perched on a stepladder and read it. Okay, I skimmed the "why" parts (something about muscles, blood, and oxygen) and paid close attention to the "how" parts, which were *enlightening*. For instance, breathing through my mouth instead of my nose would help my body get more air! I went to the lake that day and watched other runners and what do you know: mouth breathers all.

"How was your run?" John asked later.

"So much easier since I started breathing through my mouth!" I said.

He looked at me. "You've been breathing through your nose all this time?"

"I thought it would help me feel calmer."

"Oh my God," he said.

Good running shoes didn't change everything. Neither did adequate oxygen. But the two together turned me into a student of running. Soon I owned an entire shelf of running books, and I turned to them whenever something went wrong, which was always. I learned how to build stamina (grindingly). I learned to tell my gastroc from my soleus (painfully). I learned that when it feels like plantar fasciitis and heals like plantar fasciitis, it probably *is* plantar fasciitis, versus double foot cancer.

I started to see that I could start out truly awful at something and get better. Since childhood, I'd been pursuing things I was naturally good at and avoiding stuff that was hard, because if I couldn't bring home the Blue Ribbon of Parental Approval, I didn't see the point. As an adult, I pushed this reasoning even further, arguing that I didn't want to let perfectionism rule my life, so why try hard new things at all? But running was different. And I was different. I needed the experience of working hard at something just to become average at it. So I read about running. I took workshops. I tried things. I put in the miles, and over time I grew from a catastrophic runner into a mediocre one. That was *huge* for me. The beginning of my running life and the end of my drinking one overlapped by about a year, which meant that in my first days sober I was able to say to myself, "If you can run a mile, you can make it through this night without a drink." And soon, "If you can go a month without a drink, you can make it around the lake one more time."

▣

That day at the bluffs, though—there's really no technique for running up a giant sand dune other than Suck It Up. (Now that I think about it, there *may* be a codified technique for this. I will look it up.) And I am really not a suck-it-up person. I am the person who'll pay the extortionate business-class fare just to avoid sharing an armrest with a stranger. I chose my first half marathon based on the course having a net six-hundred-foot *decline*. I do, however, know how to persevere resentfully. So I did. Quads burning like nuclear rods, heart dry and gritty, leaning over my knees at every switchback to catch my breath and be unhappy—like that, I made it to the top in only twice the time it had taken me to run down.

At the top, I looked at where I'd come from. The surf was steadily pooling at least three hundred feet below me. *You came far*, I thought. *You were there. Now you're here. Just from trying. Trying, and accepting the fact that if you didn't try, you'd end up all wet. How metaphorical can one person be?* I would have liked to stand around a bit longer admiring the view and myself, but all I had to eat was a GU packet. It wasn't enough. I'd been out for longer than planned and would need another two hundred calories soon or I'd get slow and crabby. Based on the gentle roll of the terrain and my usual pace, I estimated I could be back at my car eating a banana and half a Clif Bar in twenty-four minutes. I rubbed some more sunscreen onto my face, checked that the Kinesio tape on my right knee was holding, and ran on. With less than a mile to go, I was rewarded with a close-up sighting of a bald eagle. We might have exchanged a meaningful glance.

Notes to Self: Rachel's Wedding

You can do this. You'll stay distracted. You will keep in mind that a wedding is nothing more than a big, sprawling novel. But not the one where you end up in the coat closet with Hugo and a bottle of champagne. And not the one where you drink too much red wine and spend half the reception pondering the phrase "till death do you part." And also not the one where you realize you'll probably never have that newly-in-love feeling again—or if you do, it will mean a world of trouble—and when your husband asks if everything is okay, you say, "Of course."

No. It's a different kind of novel, Russian in scope, and you'll read it and sink into it until you forget all about the trays of white wine and that hollow feeling you get when the DJ plays your high school prom theme. You will watch Rachel and Greg make terrifying promises to each other. You'll remember Harper's wedding in Indiana with eight marriages among the four parents—a whole conga line of steps and exes, affairs and lawyers and divisions of property.

That's a novel you could have read all night, if you hadn't been so tanked.

If you find yourself needing to drown in something, you'll drown in promises, broken and kept. All those promises made fifty years ago, ten years ago, three months ago. Beth and Mark got divorced within a year. Nora found out soon after her honeymoon that Jackson slept with someone the week before the wedding, and they still stayed married. Mike told Ava he'd get married when gay people could, too, and then, when it happened, he freaked out and left. Drew and Shannon had two stillborn sons in two years, and now their three adopted girls are spinning in a ring on the dance floor.

Above all you'll remember that when it becomes too much or not enough, you'll leave. Say you're sick. Say you have a long drive home. Say you're eloping with yourself. Or you'll say nothing at all and just go, a runaway bride with only one vow left. *Run*.

Permission

AFTER MARY OLIVER

You do not have to be good.

You do not have to "eat clean."

You do not have to drink hot water with lemon.

You do not have to go to your Windex-scented gym and
watch yourself run on the treadmill, wondering if
your knees really jiggle like that or if it's a trick of the
mirrors.

You do not have to use "journal" as a verb.

You do not have to look in the mirror and say you love
yourself. You do not have to love yourself. Not
today.

You do not have to go to happy hour and pretend your
club soda is a vodka tonic. You could go to the
movies. You could lie to get there; lying is fine. You
could say you have a dentist appointment and then go
to the movies and eat Sugar Babies. Or Raisinets or
popcorn or nothing.

Sugar Babies are really good, though.

The movie also does not have to be good. It only needs to
have people, or robots, or vampires who do and say
things. When it ends, you'll walk outside and it will
be dark. It will be time to go home and make dinner.
(Unless you need to see another movie. You could turn
right around and do that, too.)

You do not have to make dinner. You could eat pizza, or
just the toppings. Leftover Sugar Babies (though who
would have leftover Sugar Babies?). Bananas. Croutons.
Croutons count as dinner. The starving people of the
world will tell you croutons count.

You do not have to worry about the starving people of
the world. Not tonight. You do not have to have a
cause. If you *do* have a cause, it's okay to shed it for
now. The world won't stop making stray dogs and
child brides and sex slaves. They will be there, ready
for your help, when you are able to think about them
again.

You do not have to answer the phone or respond to
e-mail. If you do, you do not have to tell the truth to
anyone who asks how you are. Not when your truest
truth would be this:

*I feel like someone changed the angles of the furniture while I
wasn't looking. I feel like I've been dropped in Canada and
told to buy a car using only Canadian words. I feel like time
is stretching in ways that hurt my lungs and heart.*

You do not have to read good books. You do not have to
improve your mind. You could read about Jennifer
Aniston, who is either pregnant or not. Imagine being

Jennifer Aniston, standing in line to buy an açai bowl
and seeing a headline saying you're pregnant but it
still won't be enough to win back Brad. Think of the
dignity it takes to be Jennifer Aniston. No wonder she
is so taut. She is holding in the fury of all womankind.
You could think of this, but not for long, because you
might find yourself forming an army to defend her.
And you do not have time for causes.
You do not have to join Jen's Army.
You do not have to meditate.
You do not have to put lavender oil in your bath and
pretend it's a substitute for four glasses of wine.
You could sleep. You could go to bed at dusk, in a cool
room, with chocolate. You could lie there and
remember the month you spent in an Italian village
where no one spoke English. It was starkly humbling.
You were used to being confident, capable, *fluent*.
Suddenly you were reduced to smiling helplessly
and saying "Espresso me please buy?" to elderly
shopkeepers who deserved so much better. Remember
how you would gather yourself after each heart-
pounding transaction, carefully reapplying a muted
red lipstick to signify that you *were so* a sophisticated
person. One glass of Brunello wasn't enough to make
you confident, but two glasses made you stupid. There
was no right amount of wine to drink, though you
experimented tirelessly. Village Italy leveled you, as
drinking has now. But the upside to being leveled is
that it sets the bar for achievement so low. One day
you managed to buy a wedge of pecorino. Riding that

victory, the next day you bought sage leaves to fry in olive oil. *Vorrei comprare qualche salvia, per favore.* It worked! You gave him money; he gave you a bouquet of sage. Afterward, you felt like standing in the piazza and shouting *Salvia!* with your fists to the sky, an exhausted conquering hero. The next day, you bought chicken breasts. The day after that, you bought chicken breasts and had them *filleted.* Remember? And then you were elected Special American Vacation Senator. Well. The bar is even lower now.

You do not have to be good.
You do not have to regret or repent.
You do not have to say what you are grateful for.
You just have to not drink. Tonight.
You can hate it, as long as you do it.
You can close your eyes in the summer twilight, chocolate
    still coating your teeth. Angry and scared. Leveled, so
    you can rise again.

Shadow Life

A year after I got sober, I looked in the mirror and decided I had probably maxed out on the passive beauty benefits of dumping alcohol. My skin glowed, I was ten pounds thinner, and my eyes no longer screamed, *For fuck's sake somebody save me from myself.* But the worry lines between my eyebrows were as deep as ever, which seemed particularly unfair given that my actual worry level had been cut in half. *This will not stand,* I thought, and made an appointment with the best Botox injector in Seattle.

The day after my shots (by the way, the idea of having toxin-filled needles stuck in your face is way worse than the reality) I left town on a weeklong business trip. Botox takes about five days to set in, and just as promised, I woke on day five to find the sideways commas between my brows dramatically softened. I didn't look frozen or fake, just less enraged. To make sure I could still look angry when I needed to, I practiced some stern glares in the hotel room mirror and was satisfied that my eyes alone could scare a man to death.

I returned home to Seattle and waited a few days for John to notice that something had changed. By the third day, I couldn't wait any longer for the street cred I'd earned by having six shots *in my face*. "Hey," I finally asked, "have you noticed I look a little more relaxed these days?"

John looked up briefly from his newspaper. "You always look like a million bucks, babe."

"Thanks," I said. "But don't I look a little calmer, too?"

He looked at me more closely. "Yeah. I guess you do, now that you mention it." I grinned. "Wait a second," he said. Now I was beaming. "You are so sneaky. Did you go on vacation without me and just say it was a business trip?"

"No!" I said, appalled. "Oh my God. I got Botox."

John burst out laughing and then took a closer look. "Oh, yeah, I see it now," he said. "Man, they did a good job. You look like you spent a week lying in a hammock."

"I can't believe you thought I would go on a secret vacation," I said stiffly, knowing even as the words came out that it was absolutely possible. Because keeping secrets is exactly the kind of thing I do. All the time.

◻

Withholding the truth and keeping secrets are two different things. I've been doing the former since toddlerhood, because instinctively I knew that the rages and meltdowns going on in my family were things I shouldn't talk about. But my first big secret came to me when I was seven.

My father was a stoic, largely silent man. He taught computer science and spent most of his time either at the university or in his home office, with a brief, pained-seeming stop at the dinner table in between. After an hour or two in his office, he would sit in his recliner to read *Time* magazine and have a bourbon in peace. Sometimes he got that peace. But other nights, the snarled energy that had existed between my mother and me as far back as I could remember would spark into something ugly. If one of us was anxious, it spread to the other. And one of us was always anxious. My stress over, say, a playground snub could provoke an equal reaction in my mother that both justified my worry and added to it; the fear that there were no calm adults around to help me or make me feel better just made me more anxious, which spun my mom up even more. Eventually, my mother's anxiety would turn into anger at me, which took the shape of tearful yelling or hitting. From these nights I gathered that having kids was a huge mistake you had to cope with every day, and sometimes things just had to boil over.

My father generally chose not to intervene in these situations, even when they turned violent. But some nights he would get angry at me on his own—or not angry so much as deeply, righteously irritated that the quiet night and quiet life he wanted had been disrupted. He didn't know how to talk to me like a child, so instead he would ask, "Who do you think you are?" He would repeat it until he got an answer, his voice getting higher and more strained each time. I never knew what to say. I mean, who knows who they are at two years old, or four, or seven? The best I ever came up with was "just a girl" or "a person." My answer didn't really matter anyway.

We were going through this ritual one night when I was in second grade. I was frozen in my usual state, somewhere between indignation and panic, as my dad barked at me from his recliner and my mother cried into her white wine. This time, it was about a TV show I wanted to watch. Or the science fair project I didn't want to do. I can't remember. The point is that the voice inside me that usually stayed quiet during these sessions, muzzled by the knowledge that no answer would turn out well for me, suddenly spoke up and said, *I'm someone who is going to leave this place someday.*

"Who?" my father demanded. My bullheaded little self was dying to tell him exactly what I'd figured out, but I kept quiet and ended up banished to my room until morning, holding my pee until after my parents had gone to sleep and I could sneak out to the bathroom. When they'd first started locking me in my room, I would cry and beg to be let out, but my mother began putting a cassette recorder outside the door, taping my pleas and threatening to play them back when my friends came over. Now my habit was to sit on the floor hugging my knees, rocking back and forth, mumbling, "I want to go home, I want to go home." But that night I felt calm and quiet, having made contact with a secret, important part of myself my parents could never touch. From that night on our family triangle (I always saw it that way, with my sister floating amiably in the middle) gained an extra point, though no one knew it but me.

That was the beginning of a life where I always kept something back for myself. Sometimes it was out of necessity or convenience. I didn't tell my friends what my home life was really like, and I didn't tell my parents where I was really going instead of PSAT prep class. When my high school boyfriends said they loved me, I didn't let on that I wasn't even sure what love meant. But mostly it was a desire for self-preservation. A shadow life I developed to tide me over until I was old enough and free enough to build a better real one. I assumed that at some point my shadow and real lives would merge and I'd no longer keep secrets. But then the years flew by, and I guess I forgot about that plan.

Many of my adult secrets are pretty minor. For instance, when I trained for my first half marathon, I didn't hide the actual training from John or anyone else, but if a friend asked which race I'd signed up for, I'd say, "Oh, I'm not going to run an actual *race*." And it was true, at first. I had started the training plan just to see if I could learn to run 13.1 miles. But two months into training, I realized that if I did manage to run that far, I was going to want someone to hand me a goddamn medal at the end. So I found a local race where every participant got a prize and signed up for it and didn't tell anyone.

Why? It's not as if I were doing something insane or even unusual; half the people in Seattle are training for a race, climb, or triathlon at any given time. At first I thought I was protecting myself from being psyched out by doubts or horror stories. But midway through training, I knew that barring injury I would be perfectly capable of covering the distance under my own steam, even if I had to crawl parts of it. I wasn't afraid of doubt. I was afraid of encouragement. I was afraid people might wish me well and I wouldn't know what to do with their kindness. So I let them think I was running to nowhere, not toward a goal.

The one person I did tell was John, a week before race day, because I knew my cover would be blown when I got up and left the house at 5:00 a.m. on a Saturday. We were making dinner and I said, "Hey, since I've been doing so much training I thought I'd go ahead and actually run an official half. There's one in Kirkland next week, so I guess I'll check it out." Translation: *I registered for the Kirkland Subaru Mother's Day Half Marathon eight weeks ago, have closely reviewed the course map, and even drove it last week.*

John played it so cool that I suspect he was onto me. "That's great, honey. Want me to drop you off and pick you up?"

I made a face. "No need for that. I mean, thank you, though."

"Well, can I come meet you at the finish line?"

"Sure, I guess," I said. "If you *want*." A good concession on my part, because I was thrilled to see him at the race's end. And also because I was so out of it that when we returned to our cars, I walked straight past mine and tried to get into a Mazda hatchback like the one I'd owned in 1997. It was handy to have a non-delirious person with me to set me straight, though I still can't believe he let me drive.

I've also played bigger things close to my vest, having

learned in childhood that triggering someone else's anxiety could end badly for me and that the smallest thing could do it. So I'd rather keep a suspicious mole to myself than tell John or a friend and risk them freaking out on me. I also learned as a kid that making irresponsible mistakes, even small ones, wasn't okay. So when I was pulled over by the cops in my late thirties and ticketed for an expired license plate, I was so ashamed I cried when it was over. At the time, I was working sixty stress-filled hours a week while remodeling our house, raising a puppy, and drinking myself to death. But I hated myself for being the kind of person who forgot to renew her plates, and I assumed John would hate me, too.

The other teeny thing I kept from John, for a while at least, was giving up my crippling alcohol habit. It stood to reason, considering I'd hidden the habit, too, or at least that I knew the habit was an addiction. John is a hopeless optimist, especially where I'm concerned—convinced at every turn that I am desired and admired by all and destined for success. Early in my decade of serious drinking, I'd sometimes ask if he thought I drank too much. "That's ridiculous," he'd say. "You're just being self-critical."

It's true that I'd taken over my father's job of habitually searching myself for flaws and weaknesses and wondering who the hell I thought I was and why I might not deserve happiness. It's also true that I was drinking too much. But that was hard for another drinker—especially a drinker who loved me—to see. John thought I was just looking for new ways to hate myself, and I was all too ready to hear that everything was fine.

Later I'd ask the same question, and he'd say my drinking was circumstantial. *You're just stressed. We're on vacation. You had a tough day. It's your birthday.* I never pressed it. I took him at his word, the way I would believe a doctor who told me a funny-looking mole was harmless. Because John was the expert on me, right? He would know if I was changing shape or color, if my edges were blurring. The year before I quit, he finally said the words "drinking problem." We were in the kitchen and I was half-lit. "I wish I could stop worrying about my drinking," I said. By then, even when I was drunk I was worried about my drinking. John took me by the shoulders and smiled. "You have a tiny, adorable drinking problem," he said. "You'll deal with it when you're ready." Just hearing him say the words was a relief. I was an *adorable* drunk, not a grown woman operating at 40 percent power. My drinking problem was a quirk, not a threat to my life. I rode that persona for eight more months. It let me keep drinking, but it also gave me room to get to know the secret addict inside me.

I don't think it's a coincidence that John was out of town the day I woke up with a hangover and realized I was done. I had a week on my own ahead of me. There would be no one to freak me out with encouragement, to wish me well, or to watch me fail. If I needed to, I could sit on the floor and rock myself calm again, like the small animal I used to be. And I did, a little. But mostly I spent that week doing whatever nondrinking thing made the most sense to me in the moment, even if it would have looked random to someone else: walking around Lake Union after dark, alphabetizing all my books, sorting my lipsticks by color. When John arrived home the next Friday evening, I was on the sofa reading a Gillian Flynn novel, a Moroccan chicken stew cooking on the stove. "Baby!" John said, dropping his bag. "How are you?"

I stood up and walked into his arms. "I'm great," I said. "I'm six days sober."

John quit a few months after I did. It's been years now since either one of us has had a drink, and we talk about it differently. "Remember when you thought my grotesque, soul-killing addiction was cute?" I say. "Remember when I thought having three beers at lunch on a weekday was something normal people did?" he says. Now, if I'm feeling or thinking something uncomfortable, I'm liable to tell someone about it. Sometimes, anyway. I still keep some things secret. From him, from you. No one needs to know the whole story of who I think I am.

And then there was the morning of my first Brazilian wax, a longtime idle curiosity I was finally ready to satisfy. I kept that a secret from John partly to surprise him but mostly because I was terrified and knew that the slightest cringe face from him would make me back out. "I'm off for my massage," I told him on my way out the door.

"God, I need one of those," he said. "I wonder if they have any last-minute appointments. Do you have time for me to call?"

I knew he didn't have a chance in hell of getting a massage where I was going. It was a waxing-only joint. "I'm already running late," I said. "But you should get one to-morrow. I'll make you an appointment!" I beelined out the door and arrived at the shop with my heart beating sloppily in my chest. Maybe the adrenaline acted as a painkiller, because the whole thing turned out to be bearable, espe-cially once the waxer and I discovered our mutual love of 1990s Britpop. We had an animated conversation about Suede and the Boo Radleys while she held my labia with one hand and ripped the hair off it with the other. After-ward, feeling invincible and only slightly strafed from the waist down, I hugged her and drove off to meet John for lunch at a neighborhood pub. He was already in a booth, typing away on his laptop, when I slid in across from him.

"Wow, that must have been a good massage. You look seriously relaxed," he said. I just smiled. "Did you make me an appointment?"

"No," I said. "I would have, but I don't think you want what they have to offer." He raised an eyebrow. I pushed a bumper sticker from the waxing shop across the table as I slid out of the booth. "I'll just be in the ladies' room," I said, and left him staring at the words "Save a tree. Eat a beaver." In the bathroom I put on lipstick and checked my hair. I expected the knock to come in thirty seconds. It took forty-five. "Oh, hello there," I said, unlatching the door as he pushed in. "Hope you're not mad that I lied."

"Nope," he said. "Keep it up."

A Life in Liquids

TODDLER

SOUTHERN COMFORT, 1971. While your parents watch *60 Minutes*, you sit on the floor and page through *Time* magazine, stubbing your finger on any page with a bourbon ad: *Daddy drink!* Your parents find it funny but hide the magazines when your no-dancing, no-drinking Southern Baptist grandparents babysit. Your grandfather still snoops, and one day he confronts your parents by flinging open a kitchen cabinet. *What do you call* this? he demands. *I call it cereal*, your father says, because in his indignation your grandfather opened the door *next* to the one with the liquor.

TEEN

HI-C, 1974–1985. You maintain sobriety through eleven years of book reports, choir practices, family fights, and humid Floridian Christmases.

BARTLES & JAYMES, 1985. The boy looks like a surf bum version of Paul Westerberg from the Replacements. It is much easier to talk to him when you're slightly numb from the waist down, an off-label effect of strawberry wine coolers. Rolling around with him on the sand at midnight, you realize you're actually pretty good at this: the drinking, the rolling, the ocean peeing.

LONG ISLAND ICED TEA, 1986. Your prep school ID is your ticket into the gay bar where you can dance in your skimpy dresses without feeling hunted. The bartender says, *Try a Long Island Iced Tea, honey. It has everything in it but doesn't taste like any of it.* The place is a carnival of coke and amyl nitrite and synth pop. Erasure is playing tonight, but you spend the whole concert kissing your friend Michael on the balcony. *The music's boring and kissing isn't*, you tell him. *True and true*, he says. Later he'll push you in the pool with your clothes on.

ARAK, 1987. The liquor cabinet is stuffed with untouched bottles of arak and raki, anise-flavored Christmas gifts from your dad's Middle Eastern grad students. Untouched until you realize they are there. Then you sneak arak to parties in jam jars, holding your nose to disguise the taste and nearly gagging anyway. You see nothing strange about going to such lengths to consume something that repulses you. And neither does anyone else.

SCREWDRIVER, 1988. There's a Ministry show at the Lake Worth Junior High auditorium; the promoter convinced the school they're a Christian band. You get a ride with Gary, a thirty-year-old bookstore clerk who feeds you screwdrivers all night thinking he'll have sex with you later. But it's your lucky night. At 2:00 a.m., he sees the line between skeevy and criminal and stays on the right side of it. It's a line you'll learn well this last summer at home: where it lives, where it blurs, and who decides.

COED

KEG BEER, 1988. First night of college. A boy named Raven said you should come to this party. Now you stand at the closed door, unsure what to do—knock, just walk in, turn and run? A white guy with brown dreadlocks opens the door. *Hi*, he says. *Do you drink?* His name is John, and at his smile a tuning fork thrums inside you, drowning out any other words you might have wanted to say to him for the rest of the night. So you drink your beer and watch him.

JUG WINE, 1988. A student band is playing Replacements covers at a bar near campus. You are half watching them and half watching John shoot pool. You've learned things about him from mutual friends. He's a painter. He used to be a born-again Christian and spoke in tongues. He got stabbed last year with his own knife and almost died. He's writing his thesis on surrealism and phenomenology. While this last is confusing to you, the rest makes sense. He also has a girlfriend, and even if he didn't, he's clearly out of your league. It's okay. You can't speak around him anyway. So you watch him.

POPOV VODKA WITH HI-C, 1988. There's a big difference between sex with guys your own age and sex with the campus-wandering, megaphone-wielding twenty-six-year-old in your poetry class who is rumored to be AWOL from the army. Fucking someone who is aware of the existence of the clitoris is a wonderful thing. So is vodka with Hi-C, which quickly and cleanly quiets the part of you that is also kind of terrified to be with someone who has heard of the clitoris.

EIGHT-DOLLAR CHIANTI, 1989. Things did not work out with the older, crazy, rumored-to-be-AWOL poet. You have chosen a new boy your own age to fall in love with, a boy with short hair and a running car and parents. He feeds you pasta and Chianti in his downtown apartment and then fucks you in a standardized, flow-chart kind of way, where all the ifs lead to the same disappointing then. You make him mixtapes he hates. *What is this?* he says one day. The Replacements, you tell him. *They sound scraggly*, he says.

OLD-FASHIONEDS, 1990. You and your boyfriend drive across the state from the apartment you now share to his parents' beach house. Passing a rack of swimsuit calendars in a gas station, your boyfriend tells you which supermodels look good in their bikinis and which don't, and why. At the beach house you let him fuck you in the ocean, even though that's basically a terrible idea. Later, cooking dinner, you play what will turn out to be the last Replacements album. *Him again*, your boyfriend says. *If he showed up here, you'd leave with him.* You half smile. *And I'd never look back,* you say.

SIX-DOLLAR CHIANTI, 1990. You move to Florence for a year to study Renaissance poetry and drink red wine, leaving your boyfriend in the States to start grad school and further develop his philosophy of supermodels. Florence is a refined, introspective city, except for the hordes of young Italian men putting their uninvited hands on girls. *Basta!*

you learn to shout—*Enough!* Twenty years later, a man passing you on a side street in Paris will grab your breast and you will yell *Basta!* without even thinking. In Florence, you make a copy of the first Stone Roses album and mail it to your boyfriend. *This is one of the worst things I have ever heard*, he writes back.

GIN AND TONIC, 1990. You take a train to Salzburg and go on the *Sound of Music* tour. You are the only single person on the bus. Henrik the young tour guide works you into his patter: *Perhaps our beautiful American friend will marry in the cathedral where Maria married the Captain!* Everyone smiles at you and you wish to vanish from the earth. In Mondsee, there is a lunch break and you and Henrik end up in the same bar, mixing your own gin and tonics out of little silver pitchers. You are delighted by the doll-sized bar kit, and Henrik is delighted by your delight. Everyone is delighted and everyone wants to die: you because your boyfriend has breezily admitted to cheating on you with various women at grad school; Henrik because his American girlfriend has become distant and hard to reach. Henrik shakes his head and pours himself another drink. *Life is not like the movies*, he says dolefully. *Except it is a little*, you think.

GEWÜRZTRAMINER, 1990. You leave Salzburg for Bern, where you spend an entire weekend reading music magazines in cafés. From one, you learn that Paul Westerberg has quit drinking and feels great. You know you should be happy for him. Instead, you think, *We're not the same kind of person anymore*, as you drink another glass of wine and are lonely, lonely, lonely.

YUGOSLAVIAN RED, 1991. You come home from Italy and see John shooting pool in the townie bar again. His hair is shorn almost to the scalp now. *I like this*, you say, as you reach right out and buzz your hand over it. *I like that you like it*, he replies. And then you both freeze up and walk away in opposite directions. You spend most of your time that semester hanging out with his old roommate Richard, watching movies, drinking cheap red wine, and reading Robert Hass. *Longing, we say, because desire is full / of endless distances.*

SOME KIND OF PUNCH, 1991. You run into John at a party a few weeks later and panic at the sight of him. Still, you talk for hours, riding the wave of fear and desire and boozy fruit punch all the way into his bed, where you stay for a very long time. *Nothing good can come from this*, you think. You assume he won't call, but it's okay; you know things now you didn't know two days ago, things about yourself, about the world, things you can keep with you for the rest of your life. But he calls the next day, identifying himself by first and last name just in case you forgot, and asks if he can make you dinner. You sit in his tiny kitchen as he chops onions for risotto with a carbon-steel knife. You are completely at sea.

DIET COKE, 1992. You and John drive Alligator Alley, the two-lane highway connecting Florida's west and east coasts, to Miami to visit his parents. You're driving and it's daytime, so Diet Coke is the drink of choice. Brush fires blaze on the sides of the road, but as native Floridians you both find this perfectly normal. John tilts his head at the car stereo. *Who is this?* he asks. The Replacements, you tell him. He listens for another minute and says, *This is fucking amazing*, and you glow like the saw grass around you.

SANGIOVESE, 1992. John is chopping garlic in your kitchen the night Nirvana smash their instruments on *Saturday Night Live*. You are standing close to him uncorking the wine. Too close, as it happens. *Love of my life?* he says. *You're in my light.*

WIFE

PERRIER-JOUËT, 1995. You and John live in Ann Arbor with a snow shovel, a real bed with box springs, and cable TV. The day he proposes, you call your parents and say, *I have some good news*, and your mother says, *You're having a baby!* Well, no. Soon after, you visit his parents, who write your engagement date on a champagne cork and then press a penny into it. *It's an old family tradition!* says his mother. *It is?* your new fiancé says.

PERRIER-JOUËT, 1998. You buy your first house and mark the closing with champagne, pressing a penny into the cork. *It's an old family tradition*, you tell your real estate agent.

CHARDONNAY, 2000. You have jobs and insurance. You have a sofa that no one owned before you. You have a yard. You have a dog, a weird dog with emotional problems, but still. Y2K did not bring on the apocalypse. This is pretty much how life will be forever now, you think.

CHARDONNAY, 2001. Since September 11, you have been enjoying some Chardonnay almost every night, experimenting with different years and regions and developing a sense for great versus good. Though from the Internet you

come to understand that Chardonnay is considered the in-
sipid wannabe of wines, maybe because women like it.

CHARDONNAY, 2003. Aging it in steel makes it more
respectable.

CHARDONNAY, 2004. If only they could age it in gunmetal, maybe it would seem hip.

CHARDONNAY, 2005. Preferably gunmetal a bullet has
passed through.

RED STRIPE, 2006. It's time to leave the Midwest.
Really, it was time two years ago, when Bush was reelected. You idly apply for a job in Seattle and fly there in
midwinter for an interview. After the interview, you walk
down brick-paved Post Alley in a misty rain, drinking
black coffee, surrounded by green. A day later, you and
John fly to a fishing village in southern Jamaica, where an
eerie-eyed massage therapist named Shirley says, *I get the
sense you are going somewhere new. New in every way.* You open
your eyes and say, *Yes, I think I am.* Back in the cottage, you
drink a Red Stripe in the outdoor shower and pose for your
first topless photograph. *When the offer comes, let's take it*,
you say to John.

URBANITE

PINE MARTINIS, 2007. You are drunk on city life.
And on booze. You see every band you ever loved, ten
minutes from home, while drinking pine martinis served
in a frosted glass. Not the Replacements—they no longer
exist—and not Paul Westerberg, who is quiet these days
and rumored to be drinking again. But everyone else. Restaurants in your neighborhood show up in *Bon Appétit* and

Gourmet. All the movies come to town. It isn't all good; you feel crushed and terrified at your new job but hope it will pass. Outside work, though, it's a beret-tossing, martini-sipping, chef's-table frenzy.

TEMPRANILLO, 2008. Your Replacements-hating ex is in town on business and looks you up. *Yeah, okay,* you think. You, your husband, and the ex eat organ meats and tongue and drink Tempranillo in a tiny Spanish restaurant. Later, you walk your ex to his car. *Maybe our story isn't over,* he says. *I guess that depends on your definition of a story,* you say.

SAZERAC, 2008. Barack Obama is elected president. Your neighborhood pub goes off the rails with joy and disbelief and the chance to hug strangers. The next morning, wincing with a hangover but smiling, you tell John you've resolved to drink less. *If America can change, then so can I,* you say, and then you do! You change for two days.

RYE MANHATTAN, 2009. Your income has quintupled in three years. Some people would live exactly the same way as they had with one-fifth the money, and good for them. You upgrade everything, including what you drink. *We make the falernum right here,* the waiter says when taking your Manhattan order—a rye Manhattan, because you are maybe starting to grasp at straws to pretend your drinking is about ingredients and flavors. You make impressed-sounding noises. When he's gone, you ask your tablemates, *What the fuck is falernum?* No one knows. Even now, no one knows.

VARIOUS ALCOHOLS OF EUROPE AND ASIA, 2010. You visit five countries for work, having meetings that will mostly come to nothing. At night your colleagues take you out for drinks. There is a sense of fried esprit de corps. After a few rounds, your hosts open up about their seven-day workweeks and strained marriages. In Beijing, it's all this plus a side of chronic coughing. You return to Seattle exhausted, sour stomached, and resolved to drink only every other day for the rest of your life. You make it one day.

MARSANNE, 2011. Marsanne is the rye Manhattan of wines. It means you like things that are floral and round and feminine, not just drunkifying. You have a deep interest in Marsanne, in tasting it and also in drinking as much of it as possible while still keeping the wheels on. Wheels on means your head hurts every morning but your makeup is perfect and when you speak in meetings, people feel reassured and good about themselves. You suspect by now that you are no longer a real person, just a machine that drinks and lies to itself. But they don't know any better.

MARSANNE, 2012. A long boozy dinner in the East Village with people you need to impress. After dinner, more drinks down the street. After those drinks, more drinks at your hotel's rooftop bar. After that, hours on the sofa in your room staring at CNN, shaking, afraid to go to sleep because it will lead to waking up.

MARSANNE, 2013. A long dinner in Notting Hill with people you need to impress. After dinner, drinks down the street. After those drinks, more drinks at your hotel's rooftop bar. After that, hours on the bed staring out at the street, shaking, thinking about how you are slowly decaying and there is nothing you can do to stop it. And it happened *so fast*, out of nowhere. Everything was fine, and now everything is over.

· BLACK COFFEE, 2013. The next day it rains. Nauseated and light-headed, you walk along the Thames, crossing every bridge you come to. You zigzag the Hungerford and Blackfriars and Waterloo Bridges this way, listening to Paul Westerberg so you don't have to listen to your own void. *Just add water, someone's done for*, he sings. *Fuck you*, you say back. By the time you reach St. Paul's, you're drenched. You sit in a back pew, non-saint Paul in your ears, and though it will be months before you get there, in the next hour a tiny idea of the future takes shape.

TEETOTALER

SLEEP, 2013. Sleep like sky-blue water. Cascades of it.

JUNIPER SYRUP AND SODA, 2013. Juniper berry syrup tastes just like gin. Sage syrup and Meyer lemon tastes Brooklynish and smart, like a cocktail from an apothecary. Unfortunately, there is nothing in the world that tastes like a Manhattan but itself.

LEMON CUSTARD ICE CREAM, 2013. When ice cream melts, you can drink it. It's good.

GINGER-CAYENNE SHOT, 2013. Lunch at the raw vegan place with your best friend, on your hundredth day sober. *Oh, we have to try this ginger-cayenne thing!* you say. *Do we* have *to?* Mindy responds, but she's game. And after the raw vegan lunch, there's ice cream.

ROSÉ, 2014. The sight of rosé in the summer sun may always hurt your eyes.

MARSANNE, 2014. The word on a drinks menu is like

seeing an old, bad boyfriend on Facebook. Wow, he still looks great. *He was terrible for you.* Yeah, but he was fun. *You thought your life was over.* I know, but remember that thing he used to do? You know what I'm talking about. *Thirty-second dopamine explosions followed by days of gloom.* Okay, okay. But can we at least acknowledge that those explosions meant something? That there was some joy in feeling overwhelmed by them, even as they started to crush us? *Yes, okay. There was joy. Whole-body joy. Now can we close this page?* Yes. Now we can close.

SWEAT, 2015. You are fifteen feet from Paul Westerberg, trying to stay upright in the roiling concert crowd. If you stuck your tongue out, it could be anyone's sweat you'd taste. You are watching Paul as closely as you've ever watched any man. Watching to see if he's sober like you in the midst of this cyclone that he made. You think maybe yes, maybe no, and the uncertainty deflates you. Sixty–forty odds that he's at least a little drunk, you decide. Okay, seventy–thirty. And that's as close to knowing as you'll get while you stand there braced and lonely, jostled and dazed by the ecstasy of strangers. The song ends and Paul asks the crowd for requests. People start yelling names of songs, which seems to surprise him. He furrows his brow, comes to the edge of the stage, crouches down trying to hear the people in front. You are now a body's length away. Not yelling or asking for anything. Just watching. And in this moment you can say three true things about him: He looks kind. He looks drunk. And he looks scared to death.

Want Not

I had just left Babeland and was heading to my car when I spotted the otter I thought might get me sober. He was in the window of the craft shop next door, waiting to be felted into being and then hung on a Christmas tree or something. I didn't know what felting was, or even that it could be a verb. I assumed that felt, like most things, sprang from Zeus's forehead in precut rectangles, ready to rock. Apparently not. I stood on the sidewalk, looking at the otter and contemplating all the things I could learn if I got my head right, before going inside.

I had a hopeful, sheepish relationship to crafting stores. I saw them as temples to utility and skill and the concept of having an interest in something besides drinking and worrying about drinking. Twice a year I would drop mounds of cash on yarn for scarves I imagined donating to homeless shelters, or embroidery thread for tooth fairy pillowcases I would donate to children's hospitals. My crafting plans were always large-scale and philanthropic, partly to compensate the world for the wake caused by my existence but also because I needed a project. Some neo-phyte knitters might think that one scarf is a project. But then their goal is probably to make a scarf. My goal was to no longer want to drink a bottle of wine every night, and that would take *more yarn*. So I would set myself up with the needles and the patterns and the diagrams and spend about twenty minutes in earnest learning mode before re-alizing it wasn't working. I was in fact *not* absorbed in my craft, and my nerves were *not* calmed the way other knit-ters claimed theirs were, and I *still* wanted to have that glass of Viognier that would become four. And all my new sup-plies would go into the linen closet among the sheets and beach towels, to the shelf reserved for optimistic variations of myself that rarely surfaced.

That said, I had not yet tried an otter. The otter might be different. It reminded me of the one Christmas season when my mother had been absorbed in sewing ornaments from felt—judiciously sequin-studded camels, elephants, and mice. My mother was often depressed and angry. My life and sometimes my safety swung with her moods. But with a project to focus on, she was cheerful, even fun. Our house had been peaceful and easy to move through for several weeks, and decades later, when I thought of Christ-mas happiness, I still saw a felt camel in my mind's eye.

I browsed the store the way I once would have approached a man: in a slow spiral, staying off radar until I knew for sure I wanted to be seen. The store was a hodgepodge of tall shelves in narrow aisles, perfect for my cautious approach. Finally, I made my way to the rack where my otter's com-ponents hung in a take-out-style box. The label said it was perfect for people between the ages of 7 and 107. That was me! I grabbed the kit, a felting block, and a needle and hit the register. "For my niece," I told the clerk brightly, though she had not asked.

Four years later I was storing a duvet cover in the linen closet and came across my otter, still in his unmade form. I took the kit downstairs and showed my husband. "I found the otter of sobriety," I said.

John took the box and said, "I remember this guy. Are you ever going to make him?"

"It's hard to say," I said. "Just looking at him makes me feel tired. Though not as tired as he probably feels looking at me."

"True."

"I asked a lot of this otter."

"True."

I can't remember exactly what happened that night in 2010 to make my otter plan fall through. It was something good, bad, or neutral. We cooked dinner, or we went out. Maybe there was something on pay-per-view. Maybe I read a few pages of a book, maybe I got sad, maybe we fucked, maybe I did some laundry. *Something* happened to make me want to drink a bottle of wine. And wanting meant I had to. So I did.

Crafting was not my only sobriety strategy. I took a portfolio approach. Once I enrolled in a detox program where coolers of food were dropped on my doorstep twice a day. The idea was to consume no allergens, no gluten, no dairy, no sugar, no caffeine, and no alcohol for two weeks while taking "long reflective walks" (I did not do), meditating every day (did not do), and keeping a journal (dnd). I was stupefied by foodlessness and caffeine withdrawal into feeling pretty good, or at least pleasantly free from volition. On day five I remember thinking, *Maybe this is the end of wanting to drink.*

But then, on the morning of day six, I was standing on the back deck with my herbal tea when our golden retriever, Abby, fell over sideways in the backyard—stiff-legged, as if someone had tipped her over. It would have been funny if it hadn't been terrifying. For a moment I just stood there. Abby was eleven, but an active senior, still driving herself to water aerobics and her film discussion group; she wasn't supposed to just topple. Finally, I snapped to and ran to her side, yelling for John. Abby couldn't get up, so I curled my body around hers in the yard while John called the vet. She was calm and I was, too, especially the two times it seemed her heart had stopped. "It's okay if you're going," I said to her. "You just do what you need to do, baby." It didn't seem fair to beg her not to die, only to have her die anyway, thinking she'd upset me. And she did die later that day at the vet's office, a few minutes before the ultrasound that would have revealed a large, inoperable tumor on her heart.

Abby's was the first dead body I'd ever seen. She was lying on a gurney under a pink blanket, cozy and tucked in. "Oh, she looks so beautiful," I whispered. I leaned down and kissed her muzzle and her eyes and told her she was the prettiest and best girl in the whole wide world, and at the last minute I unbuckled her pink leather collar and took it home so it wouldn't be cremated with her. I sort of wish I hadn't, because seeing it in my purse a few hours later was one of the worst moments of my life.

Anyway. That was day six of the detox program, and I wanted to drink a bottle of wine that night, so I did. But it wasn't tragedy that drove my fragile flower self back to the bottle. If Abby had made it through the night, I would have gotten drunk out of worry over what the next day would bring. If she'd somehow turned out to be just fine, I would have drunk to smooth over the flow and ebb of adrenaline in my body. It's true that my dog died and it was shocking and horrible. But most days my dog didn't die. And I still wanted to drink a bottle of wine. So I did.

I bought and started giant books, so thick they had to be printed on whisper-thin page stock. I started *A Suitable Boy* four times and can report that the first twenty pages are delightful. I secretly rejoiced when I felt a cold coming on because I knew it would make me stop wanting to drink, though it really just made me want to drink a bit less. I signed up for early-morning exercise classes because I didn't think I'd show up to them hungover, but of course I did. I went on diets and wrote down everything I ate and drank to make myself more conscious of my consumption, because I thought that if I had to really face facts, I would lose my desire to drink. Not long ago, I found one of those food lists in an old Moleskine:

October 10th

Steel-cut oatmeal
¼ banana
Raw kale salad
½ chicken breast
1 apple, small
Seared tuna w/ wilted arugula
6 glasses Chardonnay

I didn't understand why I wasn't losing weight.

I asked my doctor to check my thyroid. My thyroid was fine. Blood pressure, cholesterol, liver function—fine. I had been lying for so long that my body started lying, too. "You're healthy as a horse," she said.

Other strategies that didn't make me want to stop: Smaller glasses. Switching to red. Switching to liquor. Going to therapy and talking only about other things. Yoga. Running to exhaustion. Working to exhaustion. Nature. Vacations in places so peaceful they didn't have cell signal. Puppies, rainbows, love, occasional glimpses of God in a crowd.

I did mention it to a therapist once. We got there by talking about work stress, which was linked to my propensity for taking on crushingly big jobs, which was linked to my bag-lady fears, which were linked to my impostor syndrome, which was linked to my suspicion that I was not very smart, good, or kind, which was linked to my toddlerhood and maybe infancy. "I'm *slightly* concerned about alcohol," I said to this therapist. "I'm in a rut where I need two or three glasses of wine every night just to calm down from the day." My therapist wanted to know how long that had been going on. "A while," I said.

I worked for a company that had a reputation. Everyone in Seattle knew someone who had gotten divorced, or gained forty pounds in a year, or had a breakdown or a cold that turned into hospital-grade pneumonia, or just turned hollow and brittle and paranoid. So it was easy for even skilled therapists to make false assumptions where my employer was concerned, especially when their patients were chronic and talented liars.

My therapist frowned. "That's a lot night after night," she said. "You probably could go on for the rest of your life like that, but I don't think you'd want to."

I shook my head. "I definitely don't want it to become a pattern," I said. But inside I was Ginger the dog from that *Far Side* cartoon, hearing only "You probably could go on for the rest of your life like that." Oh, how I loved her for telling me nothing had to change, that I could go on with my "two glasses" a night forever! I drank my bottle with a light heart that night.

I saw a psychic who smudged me with sage and told me things about myself that made my neck prickle, but she didn't mention my drinking. I saw a hypnotherapist who tilted me back in a puffy recliner and put me in a trance. I did 108 sun salutations on the darkest day of the year to bring some light back to my soul. And nothing made me stop. Because I didn't want to stop drinking. I wanted to stop *wanting to drink*. Because then the stopping itself would be as easy as avoiding spin class or olives or pointy-toed shoes or Ryan Reynolds movies or anything else I didn't like.

In the end, the way I stopped was by stopping. I woke up one Saturday in June with a wine headache. My husband had left before dawn on a business trip, so I lay alone in our king-sized bed in the miserable sunlight contemplating a whole day having to move my head around on my body, and something in me said, "Okay. Okay, I get it." Suddenly I understood that what I wanted was no longer important. I would just have to wait and hope that eventually I would want something else.

I got out of bed and took Advil and went to Pilates and then met my friend Mindy for lunch at a hip new barbecue restaurant in a hard-to-get-to, harder-to-park-in corner of town where we proceeded to eat salads with no barbecue elements whatsoever. She had most of the dirt on me, and she knew I wanted to cut back. But that day, when she asked about my plans for the evening, all I said was "Relax and enjoy the quiet, I guess."

"Isn't it amazing when husbands go out of town?" she said, and I agreed that it was pretty great.

It was, in fact, lucky that my husband was out of town that day because I wanted to face this alone. I had read about the "pain cave" that ultradistance runners go into, and I had also seen *Trainspotting* and *Drugstore Cowboy* and *Jesus' Son* and all the other heroin movies. I didn't expect to face any kind of physical horrors, but what awaited otherwise, I didn't know. Many nights I had tried to wait twenty minutes between wanting a glass of wine and having one and almost always failed. So that was my starting point: I was a grown, multi-degreed, loved, moneyed, professionally powerful woman who did not have the strength to wait one-third of an hour before having a drink. And all the therapy and hypnosis and diets and Reiki (did I mention the Reiki?) hadn't helped.

But the difference was that I'd been trying to kill the want. And now I was just saying no to it.

Still, I thought it might get ugly and was glad to be alone to gut it out. I kept myself busy all afternoon, and when I finally got home, I was girded with magazines and chocolate and ideas for movies to watch and everything else you bring your friend when she breaks up with her boyfriend. I hunkered down and waited to fall apart.

Things were fine until around 9:00 p.m., when I would normally decide to have one glass of wine. I was loading the dishwasher when I noticed the time and then, on cue, the wanting. My heart beat in a creepy, sloshy way. I put down the plate I was holding and leaned against the butcher block and then slid down to my haunches, because why not? If I could have, I would have liquefied the flagstone tiles, buried my feet in the muck, and remade them around me to hold myself to the earth. *Think of all the times you haven't had something you've wanted*, I told myself. Houses, jobs, men. A Jean-Paul Gaultier clutch that snapped together with brass knuckles. A happy childhood. I'd missed out on all these things and lived. I could lose this and live, too.

I stayed low for another minute, crouched down on my

kitchen floor, feeling sorry for myself over the clutch and the houses and the people who'd failed to fall in love with me even though I was clearly amazing. The self-pity calmed me down enough to eventually rise back to counter level and finish loading the dishwasher. It was 9:15.

How did I spend the rest of the night? I walked around my house looking at stuff. I went up to the third floor and looked out the window where we could see the Space Needle in winter, when the trees were bare. Now it was June and the leaves were on the trees, so I looked at the leaves. Matthew Barney's *Cremaster Cycle* book was open on the sofa and I flipped through it for a minute, but it was kind of gross, so I put it back on the shelf and had dark thoughts about my husband's taste in art.

On the second floor we had a collection of small Czech pots and vases that my in-laws had given us over the years. I picked them up one by one and examined the signatures and dates etched on their bottoms. Sixty years ago, people in gray postwar Czechoslovakia had made these beautiful, nominally functional little vessels by hand. They must have been brave, focused, *sober* people, I decided. Unlike me, they must have had purpose and stout hearts and belief in the future. Unlike me, they did hard things and ate sensible foods and slept heavy as sandbags at night.

I stood in the hallway comparing myself to the great saints of mid-century Czechoslovakia for a while, and then I went into the bathroom and practiced doing a smoky eye.

That's how the evening passed, the first of my sobriety— with wandering and wanting and saying no. I had expected to be wide awake all night, but by midnight I was exhausted.

I slid into bed and lay on my side thinking about the night. It had been manageable, I realized. Manageable was beyond my wildest dreams. Managing was something I could probably do two nights in a row. As for how people managed not to drink for millions of nights in a row—thinking about that made my heart flop around, but I assumed it was a matter of skill and practice. I had once not known how to manage an emergency, or a difficult meeting, or a home renovation, and now I did. Maybe I could learn to subvert my own wants the same way—with processes and contingency plans and occasional meltdowns.

On the nightstand was a matte blue Czech dish for my lip balm and earplugs. I reached over and touched it now. *I can be like you guys*, I thought. Stolid and Soviet. Not once did it occur to me that my wants could be transformed. Faith was something I told other people I had in them. But toughness and will I understood. Grow up with nothing but a few sequined felt camels standing between you and your mother's anger, and you will be tough, even if it looks to others like fear. I knew I could be tough for a very long time.

I slept for ten hours and woke in a greenish rainy light. Outside the trees were fretting in the wind. I lay still in the middle of the bed, feeling suspended in my own body and wanting nothing but what had just happened: to make it to my second day without a drink. *You have a whole morning ahead*, I thought. *You can do anything.*

Do You Have a Drinking Problem?

1. Do you drink every day?

☐ Yes

☐ No

2. Do you frequently have more than one drink in a day?

☐ Yes

☐ No

3. "One drink" is

☐ Five liquid ounces.

☐ Five liquid ounces, plus any top-ups made when no one is looking.

☐ It depends on how unfairly the world has treated me that day.

☐ Measurement is a bourgeois and even patriarchal construct.

4. Has your drinking ever led to someone seeing you naked who maybe shouldn't have?

☐ Yes
☐ No
☐ Fuck you with your shoulds and shouldn'ts.

5. *The "5:00 a.m. fear" is*
☐ Waking up from a nightmare at 5:00 a.m.
☐ Waking up when the booze wears off, knowing you messed up again, like you mess up every night.
☐ I don't like you.

6. *Are you very proud of times you* don't *drink? Before five, at business dinners, when you have the flu, when you're visiting your fundamentalist grandma who lives in a dry county? Do you feel pretty goddamn special about setting this one limit?*

7. *What five words describe how tired you are?*

8. *Have you ever lied to the following people about your drinking?*
☐ Doctor
☐ Shrink
☐ Spouse
☐ Mother
☐ Hairdresser

9. *You lie to your hairdresser?*
☐ Yes
☐ Maybe
☐ She has too much power over me already.

10. The sexual choices you make while drinking are
☐ More dubious than the dubious sexual choices you make while sober.
☐ Less dubious than the dubious sexual choices you make while sober.
☐ Wouldn't you like to know?

11. Has anyone ever suggested you cut down on drinking?
☐ Yes
☐ No
☐ Why, what have you heard?
☐ Do assholes count?

12. What five words describe your fear at this moment?

13. When other people leave wine in their glasses, you
☐ Finish it when they're not looking.
☐ Get annoyed because you can't refill yours until they finish theirs and you really need to refill yours.
☐ Want to cry because some people are obsessed with astronomy or civil rights or God, and you're obsessed with this.

14. Have you ever tried and failed to quit drinking?
☐ Yes
☐ No

15. Did you fall down the first time you tried to walk?
☐ Yes
☐ No

16. *When you fell down, did you ever get back up?*
□ Yes
□ No

17. *Are you sensing a subtle metaphor?*
□ Yes
□ No
□ Subtle?

18. *One year from today your first waking thought will be* ____
_____.

19. *Five years from today you will spend your nights* _____
_____.

20. *When you set this fear down, you will pick up* _____
_____ *in its place.*

Cat got your tongue? That's okay. This quiz has no time limit. Those blanks will still be there when you figure out what goes in them.

Going Long

"Fatigue?" my shrink, Carol, says.

"A little."

"Physical pain?"

"None." In truth, I stepped wrong on the trail yesterday and my ankle's a little crabby, but she doesn't need to know that. She gets in my face ever since I ignored weeks of sharp shin pain while training for a half marathon and it landed me in an ortho boot for two months.

"Anger?"

"A little." It's a standard inventory we go through every week. A list of life elements to which I answer, "Lots," "Some," "A little," or "None." Depression, anxiety, fatigue, pain, anger.

Grief, competence, pleasure? *Some, some, some.* Would I know I was grieving if someone didn't ask me? I'm not sure. Would you? Try it. Set an alarm once a week and ask yourself what you've lost.

"Suicidal thoughts?"

"None." Never. By the time I was ten, both my parents

had threatened suicide in front of me. *You make me want to put a gun to my head.* It inoculated me against any personal interest in that path.

"Hopelessness?"

"None."

"That's good." She writes something on her legal pad while I watch the late-afternoon sun bounce off the Space Needle.

"I mean, *futility*, yes," I say. She looks up. "But in, like, a Sisyphean sense. I wouldn't call it hopelessness per se." She raises an eyebrow. " 'Hopelessness' is a very specific word," I explain.

"Maybe we should come back to this," she says.

▣

Later that week I drive to a park near Kirkland to watch people run the Pigtails Challenge, a 200-mile trail race. To be fair, only the crazy people are running all 200 miles; the normal ones are just doing 100 or 150. The course is a 10-mile loop of packed dirt, so you run it once, and then again and again until your life is over. The first time I ran a half marathon, at the end of mile one I thought, *See, that was easy, and you only have to do it twelve more times!*—a thought I immediately regretted. I imagine some of the Pigtail runners finish the first loop, say *Only nineteen more!* to themselves, and then tear their clothes off and spin around in circles, weeping.

The Pigtails Challenge is so long and hard that, as with many ultramarathons, you're allowed to have people run parts of it with you. Officially, they are meant to help you stick to a certain pace, but any ultra-runner will tell you it's also about helping you keep your shit together in the later stages of the race. At least that's how our friend pitched it to my husband when he asked him to be his pacer in miles seventy through eighty: "I just need you to talk to me and help me go slow enough."

"I can talk and be slow," John said. And now they're out there together, somewhere on the Lake Youngs Watershed. I've driven here to cheer them on, but I might not even get to see them—so much depends on when the friend started, how fast he's going, how long I stay. And it doesn't much matter, because I'm not really here to be a fan. I'm a tourist: I came to see what futility looks like and how people go on once they've figured out there's no point to going on.

I've only run big races with corporate sponsorship. Those have a slicker vibe, with massage tents and shoe-sensor timing and kids' dashes and all the free glucose gel you can stand. This is not that. This is a few rented tents, a whiteboard for tracking time, and half a dozen people, mostly lanky forty-something guys in fleece, grilling hot dogs. The only way I'm sure I've arrived at the right place is the large electronic clock that says this race started twenty-six hours ago. I wouldn't even think they had a permit except that one guy says, "Should we get out the beer at some point?" and another guy replies, "Yeah, except I told King County we weren't bringing beer, so let's wait till dark."

It's a typical late-spring Seattle day: gray, cool, and drizzly. Perfect running weather but less ideal for standing around watching. I have a mild case of Raynaud's syndrome, meaning one of my arteries sometimes freaks out in cold weather, and one or more fingertips turn deathly white. It's happening with my right index finger now, so I grab a cup of hot water at the tent to warm it up. I wait for someone to ask who I am and what I'm doing there; I am always sort of waiting for people to ask who I am and what I'm doing there, even at the movies or the grocery store. But they just smile and say, "Hey."

I smile back and wander to where the trail emerges from the woods, on the lookout for human suffering.

I expect the first sufferer to be white, sinewy, and sort of Jesus-y looking like the guys in the tent, because that's mostly what I see on my own trail runs, not to mention in the streets, offices, restaurants, and retail establishments of the entire Pacific Northwest. But it's a robust black woman in her forties, and she's *smiling*. "Hey, girl, hey!" she calls out to the tent dudes as she jogs up.

"Hey, girl, hey!" the tent dudes call back. She hangs out for about ten minutes, eating pretzels and chatting about the new truck someone just bought, then heads back out while we clap. She's so cheerful and energetic that I think it must be early in her race. But no: "Just three laps to go!" the keeper of the whiteboard calls after her. That means even if she's only running the hundred-mile distance, she's seventy miles in. I am a stoic animal who hides her pain, and even I would have stopped hey-girling by mile sixty.

My second chance to see a human being struggle not to implode in the face of nothingness comes a few minutes later. This woman is poker-faced and less chatty than the first. She visits the Porta-John, grabs a handful of potato chips, and gets right back on the trail. "Hey, you forgot to ask my race number!" she calls over her shoulder to the timekeeper.

"Oh yeah, what's your number?" the timekeeper asks, though he's already jotted down her time.

"867-5309," she sings, and disappears around the bend.

What is up with these people? I think. *Do they not understand that this is a desperate situation?*

⬚

"Tell me more about the futility," Carol says.

I pick up a throw pillow and clutch it on my lap. "Well, let's say I finish writing this book and it does okay."

She nods. "You publish a successful book."

" 'Successful' is a complicated word," I say. "Let's just say it earns enough money that the publisher wants another one." Carol nods in assent, or at least acceptance. "Then I'll have to write another one."

"I thought you wanted to write another one," she says.

"Oh, I do. But that's not the point," I say.

"Okay," Carol says.

"And then there's my job. I'm enjoying it. I feel genuinely valued. It's going well."

She smiles. "Certainly sounds that way."

"But what happens when you do well at work?" I ask her. "They ask you to do *more* work. That's the *best-case* scenario. Like the best-case scenario for writing a book is writing another book. Like the best-case scenario for running is you don't get hurt and you can keep running."

Carol leans forward a little. "But unless something has drastically changed, you *love* all these things."

"I do," I tell her. "But isn't it kind of horrific that they just go on and on and on? And then, you know, after that I'm going to *die*."

▣

I was a death-obsessed child. I bruised easily, and the cancer-kid stories in *Reader's Digest* always started with mysterious bruises. I'd read them and go to my mother with a lump in my throat and tell her I was worried I might have cancer. "Worrying about something won't stop it from happening," she'd say, "so you might as well not worry." Which, in her defense, might have been great advice to give to another adult, but not an eight-year-old.

I got sick a lot, too—missed weeks of school with bronchitis and tonsillitis and stomach pain that crystallized my entire being into a single abdominal knot. Getting sick for real was a relief because how could I come down with cancer when I *already had something else?* Also, my mother was extra nice when I was sick, bringing me *Archie* comics from the drugstore and letting me watch talk shows all day. She got sick a lot, too, so it was nice to finally have something in common.

By the time I was in middle school, I worried less about dying slowly from cancer and more about being vaporized in a nuclear war. This fear peaked around the time *The Day*

After aired on television. I was much too scared to watch the film, but I read everything I could find about it to learn exactly how I could expect to die and how long it would take and how much it would hurt. Every time I went outside, I looked up into the clear blue Florida sky for missiles. Finally, I broke down and asked my mother if she thought maybe South Florida, being remote from the rest of the country, might be unharmed in a nuclear war. "There's not a damn thing I can do to stop a nuclear war, so I just don't think about it," she said.

"Okay, but thinking about it now, do you think we'd be all right?" I pleaded.

"I have no idea, but I know worrying about it won't stop it from happening," she said.

Sometimes when I was at the public library reading up on nuclear war, I would also take a few minutes to research Alzheimer's disease. My mother's mother had been diagnosed in her early fifties and was by then in a nursing home, dying. *Time* magazine said the early-onset form might be hereditary. I wondered how long it would be until my own mother became confused and then hostile and then violent and then pale and skeletal and shadowy. I couldn't ask her, so I returned obsessively to the same news articles, looking for the line I'd missed that said, "Oh, but of course none of this will ever actually happen," or "But of course a cure is mere weeks away." I made up an escalating strain of early-onset Alzheimer's whereby my mother would be struck in her forties and then me in my thirties. I could spend hours almost physically frozen, imagining what it would be like to lose my mind in my thirties—an old age, yes, but *young*-old.

Fortunately, by the time I was sixteen, I'd figured out that alcohol was the cure for all of my anxieties, and I stopped worrying so much about cancer and dementia and vaporization. It wasn't until college that an agonizing death from AIDS came to seem like an inevitability, because I was having sex with a few different guys and only using condoms 98 percent of the time. I had read a story in *People* magazine about Alison Gertz, a young white woman from an affluent family who had gotten AIDS through a single heterosexual encounter. If it could happen to her, it definitely *would* happen to me, I reasoned. I also got it into my head that bad sex raised the likelihood of contracting AIDS, though if that were true, young women worldwide would have been dropping like flies. I walked around for months fairly sure I was HIV positive but terrified to get tested or even talk to a doctor about it. After all, there was no cure. There was barely a treatment. My best option for not dying was simply to refuse to acknowledge it.

Once I'd finished school, picked just the one best guy to sleep with, and moved a thousand miles away from my parents, my health terrors gradually faded. If you don't count the anthrax and smallpox and super-flu episodes that sent me to the Internet for face masks and gloves and black-market Cipro, all of which still occupy a shelf in my utility closet. Because you never know. Alcohol helped to bury those terrors, too, as long as I paid close attention to the articles about wine *preventing* heart disease and ignored the ones about wine *causing* heart disease, plus cancer, depression, and liver failure.

My eventual sobriety, which I'd imagined would feel like a lifelong panic attack, turned out to be more like ripping off a giant Band-Aid: a moment of searing pain followed by wonder that I'd ever thought I needed that much protection. Now I rarely worry about the manner of my death, though I still take issue with the fact that it has to happen at all.

▣

Finally, someone who fits my vision of an ultra-runner emerges from the woods—over fifty and well over six feet tall, with brown dreadlocks to his knees and retractable hiking poles strapped to his waist. He's wearing the minimalist shoes that are supposed to be like running barefoot and has tattoos on the backs of his astonishing, tree-trunk thighs. At the aid tent, they ask what he wants to eat. I wait for him to pull a chewed-up root out of his shorts and say, *I am nourished by the spirits of the trees.*

"How about something to make me run faster, not feel pain, and be in a better mood?" he says. "A steroid smoothie, maybe."

"We have pizza," the guy manning the grill says.

"Even better!"

While the dreadlocked guy is eating, a woman comes in and heads straight to a white tent set up away from the others. "I'm going to sleep for a couple of hours," she calls.

Before she zips herself in, I see four white cots lined up inside.

Another man appears, the first person I've seen all afternoon who is full-on running rather than shuffling or jogging. He's also the first one who doesn't stop to eat, pee, or rest. "RUNNING SUCKS BALLS!!!" he yells as he flies past us.

The dreadlocked guy chews and swallows. "It's hard to argue with that," he says to no one in particular.

Over the next hour I start noticing that almost every runner is walking kind of funny. Their arrivals and departures are slow even by my standards. Aid-tent breaks seem downright leisurely, but no one sits down. I ask someone why and am told it's for fear of never getting back up. I also learn that the trekking poles are for walking the uphills.

Wait. Walking the uphills? That counts? I walk sometimes during my runs and races, but I thought that just meant I sucked. Later, I ask an ultra-runner friend about this. "Well, yeah," he says. "You have to pace yourself. You can't just barrel through."

"That's not how I've been doing it," I say. My version of pacing is to run hard and fast until I can't anymore, then walk to recover, then run hard and fast until I can't anymore (which happens faster each time), and so on.

Early in my running career—which is the wrong word, it's more like a running internship—I said to this same friend, "When I'm running, I basically cycle through the five stages of grief over and over in my mind."

He laughed. "You're doing it wrong."

"I don't know how to do it right!"

"You'll figure it out."

"Why don't you just tell me, Yoda?"

I had assumed people who ran a hundred-mile race would be preternaturally in tune with their bodies and minds. But everything I've seen today says they're just good at adapting to conditions. They do what works, whatever and whenever that is.

I think back to my first six months sober and how clear it became that I needed my life to not, as the man said, suck balls. It hit me within weeks that I needed a happier job, more practice saying no, more sleep, more time outside. More time in general, for walking the uphills.

And it felt futile. The notion of stacking up sober day after sober day until the occasion of my funeral felt fucking pointless. All that effort, just to die. I didn't know then that eventually I'd stop stacking days. That I'd just be living a life. That I wouldn't have to pay close attention to every root and rock on the path in front of me. That I'd be sure-footed enough to also notice the trees and the wind and even the occasional owl and to realize that both time and space were far denser than I ever knew.

Carol can't really argue with the fact that I'm going to die, though she looks as if she might like to. "Yes, after writing lots of books and running lots of miles, you'll die someday. We all will," she says.

I shrug. I have decided to prioritize worrying about my

own death over the death of everyone else except for close family members, my dogs, and, for reasons I don't fully understand, Michael Stipe.

"Do you think you're going to die young?"

"Not really, but I guess it depends what 'young' means."

She stares at her bookshelf for a moment. I think she might be looking for a heavy book to hurl at me, but when she speaks again, she speaks softly.

"You are perilously close to having the life you've always wanted," she says. "It's not surprising to me that you would panic."

"I know," I say as I grip the throw pillow tighter. "I know."

For thirty years I watched my mother closely for signs of dementia. Dropped words, illogical statements, a tendency to jump wildly from topic to topic. "I think it might be starting," I'd say to John, who would respond gently, "I think it might just be how your mother *is*."

Two years ago, my parents were at our house for dinner, and my grandmother came up in conversation. "I'm so relieved you didn't get early-onset Alzheimer's, too," I said to my mother.

"Oh, Mother didn't have that," my mom said. "Didn't we tell you?"

"No?" I said.

"She had Pick's disease," my father said. "It has the same symptoms, but it's not genetic. Well, not usually."

"How do you know this?"

"From the autopsy," my dad said. "I'm sure we told you this."

"You did not tell me this," I said, staring across the table at John.

"It doesn't sound familiar," John piped in.

"Huh," said my father. "I guess we just forgot."

"For thirty years I have been waiting for a devastating genetic brain disease to strike Mom, then me," I said.

"I really thought we'd told you," my mother said. "Sorry, baby."

"I guess we just figured you would know," my father said.

After dinner, John and I wave in the driveway as my parents drive off. When they're gone, he turns to me and says, "I guess they just figured you would know," and we laugh so hard we can't talk.

While I'm texting a friend and distracted from the race, John finishes his pacer loop. I find him eating a Clif Bar at the aid tent. "Oh, hey," he says casually. He seems pretty chipper for someone who just ran ten miles. "It was great," he says. "I think I could do another one. I mean, literally another *one*." His friend is already back out there alone, with thirty miles to go.

"I think part of me thought you were going to have a heart attack and die," I tell him.

"I know, baby," he says.

It's raining for real now, and at home the dogs are waiting for dinner. John walks me to my car and sees the bag I keep there with a set of running clothes and my second-best shoes, for times I'm seized by the urge to head out. That bag has saved me from drinking, panic, yelling at John, upending a conference table. Once I start moving, everything trapped in my head flows into my body, where there's space for it to soften and diffuse. It's still mildly shocking to me that my body can take on the pain of running and the pain of my thoughts and thrive. Maybe all those years I was waiting for it to fall apart, it just needed a job to do. "It seems like if we can, we should," a friend once said about running. That's what I come back to when I find myself slogging down a muddy trail or up a steep hill, thinking, *Why are you doing this?* Because I can. Because for now, my legs are willing.

"There's twenty-four hours left on the clock," John jokes when he sees my bag. "Not too late to join." *No way*, my brain says. But my body says, *Can we, pretty please?* and calls to me through sense memories: the tug of my ponytail, the damp air on my bare legs, the ache between my shoulder blades that sets in when I go long and my rhomboid muscles decide for no reason that they can help. *Impossible*, my brain says, but my body is craving the tedium and pain and possibility of good cheer out there on the hamster wheel, where I belong.

Notes to Self:
Neil Finn Concert

This will be easy. Just give up any expectations of being transported, moved, or even entertained. Place your drink-less body in front of the stage and just stand there and watch Neil Finn.

Of course it's hard to imagine because you've never done it. On the way to your very first show you drank strawberry wine coolers in your friend's car. You weren't much of a drinker yet, but a live show was too high stakes to deal with straight. And you were *supposed* to be uninhibited at a concert. At least that's the impression you got from MTV. The concert was a letdown (Stipe was in a mood), but you didn't care, because the alcohol unfroze your body below the neck, let it buzz and even move a little.

Based on this one data point, you drank at shows for the next thirty years. All those plastic cups. All that time spent in line at the bar and in horror-show restrooms, because your bladder was never meant to hold so much liquid. If you're honest, the timing of drinks and pees is your main memory from those nights, not the ecstasy or force of any-

thing happening onstage. Alcohol didn't kill your inhibi-
tion, it just muffled it, and the moments of surprise that
snuck through the scrim could be uncomfortable (like when
Mark Eitzel got so nervous mid-show that it seemed he
might flee the tiny stage) or scary (like the hour alone
searching for a cab in the Castro at 2:00 a.m.).

This will be easier. You won't have to calibrate your
bladder capacity. You won't be drunk or hanging out
with drunks, so you won't have to deal with the messy
postshow comedown. Not like the last time you saw Neil
Finn play, a decade ago in Chicago. You went with Miles,
whose girlfriend had just left him. You drank a lot; Miles
drank more. Afterward you went to a hipster dive bar that
was so packed you sat on the bench of an old baby grand
in the back room. You were starting to sober up, but he
drank a bunch more beers, quickly, determinedly. He
wouldn't talk, only wanted to pick out "Don't Dream It's
Over" on the piano. But every time you made a move to
leave, he grabbed your wrist and said, "You have to stay.
You have to." You knew that when his girl left she took
the bed, the sofa, and everything in the kitchen except a
plate and a fork. So you stayed. And when he finally started
talking, you listened.

"I cry a lot," he said.

"Crying is fine," you said.

"The romantic part of my life is over for good," he said.

"You're young," you said. "It's barely getting started."

"I might be a monster," he said.

"Stop it," you said, and he picked up your hand and
kissed it. He looked you dead in the eye and said, "Then I'm

a ghost," with such finality that you didn't argue. And in the years to follow, he did become a ghost of sorts, detaching from love, then hope, then conversation. Eventually, he drifted from you, too, whom he'd once said he felt bound to for life. Sometimes you wonder if you missed the moment to say, *Enough with the drunken metaphors. You are in an ordinary human mess that can be fixed.* But that's a sober thought. Drunks love big talk, and that night you were full of it.

Except for Neil Finn, tonight will be different in every way. No beers, no piano, no Miles-ghost to drag back to earth. Though you would try, if he ever turned up next to you again. *Hey now, hey now*, you'd say. *Let's start very small. Let's stand in one place while this man plays a song, and then we can look for the next right thing to do.* But he's not here and he won't be. So say it to yourself instead.

Girl Skulks into a Room

I am not a joiner. Worse, I'm a leaver. I love that rush of front-porch vacuum quiet when the door to a party shuts behind me. I love leaving group dinners just before someone orders dessert and drags out the whole godforsaken thing another thirty minutes. I've been known to get to the intermission of a play and say, "Well, I think I've got the gist of it by now." There's only so much I can take of you people and your celebrations and that thing where you want me in your life. It's a lot, okay?

So when I tell you I went to my first AA meeting at eighteen months sober because I was so lonely I thought I might disappear, you know it was serious.

It took me nearly that long to realize I was lonely. First I had to pass through the just-got-sober part, where I was safest holed up at home with a cozy mystery and vats of ice cream. Then there was the wonderment phase, where I realized that the vaguely tired feeling I'd had for years had actually been a constant low-grade hangover and that I *never had to have one again*. Soon after that I got serious about running, as the newly sober are prone to do, and, well, it's hard to be lonely when you're focused on not letting your body collapse and die on a hilly trail. Sometimes I would run with Terry Gross in my ear, but even she could get tiresome with her incessant *questions*. Often I would just enjoy the feeling of having a body that I wasn't actively destroying from the inside out.

At some point after that, sober life just became *regular* life, and I was both thrilled and comforted to be living at ground level, instead of alternately high above and below. The social culture at my job was a boozy one, and I got off the happy hour hamster wheel with relief. My circle of close friends got smaller and tighter and dearer to me. I wandered and read and looked at the path that had gotten me into trouble. Everything seemed just fine. Then, one mild summer afternoon, I passed two twentysomething women on a bench outside Cafe Allegro. I heard the one with a crew cut and tattoos say, "The thing is, a lot of those people didn't know me before I got sober."

It was all I could do to not run over and sit in her lap: "You're sober? Oh my God, me, too! Do you want to sit here and talk about it all day? Because I totally will if you will. I know I'm nearly twice your age, but I can still be your best friend, I promise. Please, please just let me sit here and talk to you about being sober."

Even after I was safely settled inside the café, I couldn't stop watching those girls through the front window, especially when they laughed. I wanted to be with them so badly that tears came to my eyes and I realized that I was desperately lonely. I had friends on the Sober Internet, but no one to sit with on an actual, physical bench and swap stories. Occasionally, I would try to share something with a real-life friend: "I can't believe I did _____," or "I used to _____ and lie about it," or "Remember that time I said _____? It was actually _____." And the friend would generally respond by saying either "Well, that's not so bad" or "Yeah, but everyone does that." Then I'd feel even lonelier, because I'd tried to explain just how bad it had gotten and not been heard.

It's true that as far as public alcoholic antics go, mine weren't particularly exciting. I told secrets (mine and others'). I drove when I shouldn't. I closed down bars on several continents and put myself in risky or just inane situations. I didn't wreck my car, or get arrested, or fuck other people's husbands. But the more sober time I racked up, the more clearly I saw that those unimpressive fuckups and lost evenings had been acts of aggression against myself. I'd hurt myself over and over. And I realized this was something only a fellow traveler, someone else who'd made it to the other side, could fully understand. That day at the café, as I pressed on my eyes to shove the tears back in (this doesn't work, by the way), I thought, *I need to find my people. Sober people.*

But how? Meetup came to mind, but it involved, you know, meeting up with people. Also, it was based on hobbies, and as a drinker I really didn't understand the notion of shared interests (besides drinking) bringing people together.

I told John, "I need to figure out a way to meet other sober people."

"That sounds simple enough," he said.

"You think?" I asked. "I'm not sure where to start. I think I need, like, a Meetup group, but for alcoholics. I guess I could check their website."

He gave me a funny look. "Sure. Or, you know, AA?"

Oh. *Right.*

And that's how, a mere five months later, I found myself standing outside a Presbyterian church in a tweedy, old-money corner of North Seattle. Well, first I was sitting in my car outside the church, and then I was standing next to my car, and then for a few minutes I was back in it, looking up movie times on my phone. My head felt light and my mouth was almost entirely out of spit. *Scared spitless,* I thought. The church complex was large, and I watched people come and go through various doors. I knew there was no such thing as "looking like an alcoholic," but still, I was disappointed that none of them looked like alcoholics, which would have made it easier for me to pre-assess them for friend potential and maybe weasel out of the whole deal.

Except I didn't weasel or slither anymore. Not much, at least. *You did the hard part a long time ago,* I told myself. *You can walk into a room and sit in a goddamn chair.* I got out of the car and walked to the nearest entrance. A small wooden sign with AA carved in it hung from the doorknob. *Yeah, but I don't want to walk in there,* I said to myself. *You don't have to want to,* I said back. *You just have to do it.* And in I went.

I had researched local meetings on the AA website. This one was labeled as women only and as a speaker meeting, meaning most of the time would be devoted to one person telling her story. I'd decided, based on nothing, that there would be lots of people in attendance. So my plan was to slip in, sit near the back, make as little eye contact as possible, keep my mouth shut, and hightail it out the moment the meeting ended—like auditing a college lecture. The friend-making part of my plan would commence later, once the mute and stealthy phase was over.

Of course, I didn't know then that the AA meeting directory is not known for being particularly accurate or up to date. But I started to get a clue when I walked into a room with one large round table, occupied by an older man who looked kind of like Jerry Orbach from *Law & Order.* "Hello there, young lady!" he said, smiling. "If you're looking for the Ladies' Halloween Festival Committee, it's next door."

I have never, ever wanted anything as much as I wanted to say yes, I was looking for the Ladies' Halloween Festival Committee. And I'm sure they could have used an extra lady to help make candleholders out of miniature pumpkins or whatever. But I was already answering, "No, I'm here for the AA meeting?" with that girly upswing in tone. He looked surprised, which in itself surprised me, because I figure *anyone* you see on the street could be an alcoholic, and it seemed as if he ought to know that even better than I did. But he recovered fast, introduced himself, and showed me to the coffee and cookies.

While I was helping myself to coffee to jack up my nerves a little more, a young woman in a hoodie arrived and greeted Jerry as though they'd known each other longer than she'd been alive. "Just trying out a new meeting?" she asked when we were introduced, and my inner voice hissed, *Say yes! Say you are a Chicago-area radiologist visiting Seattle for a conference on radiology innovations and just checking out a new meeting for fun.* But my outer voice went rogue and said, "No, this is my first meeting ever, actually." That got their attention, especially when I added that I'd been sober for a year and a half. "Wow, you sure picked a rough way to do it," the girl said, and Jerry heartily agreed. *Okay, whatever, Kool-Aid drinkers*, I thought, but I couldn't sustain the bitchiness for very long, because they were both so nice.

In all, eleven people gathered at the round table. At least half of them were retirement-age guys, including an emeritus professor who deeply impressed me with his casual use of the word "attenuated." Aside from the young girl, the rest were a mix of men and women around my age. They all seemed to know one another pretty well. I felt as though I'd barged into a private gathering of old friends—not because anyone's behavior even remotely suggested that, but because I habitually feel like I've barged into a private gathering of old friends, and this situation was perfectly structured to throw that feeling into high relief. When Jerry introduced me at the start of the meeting and I was welcomed with big smiles, I thought to myself, *They don't really want you here. They're just being nice because they're afraid you'll go have a drink if they aren't.* As if that would be so bad, for strangers to be kind to stop me from hurting myself. As if I would be taking something they couldn't afford to give.

So there I was, a stranger at a table of old friends. A defensively dressed and made-up forty-four-year-old woman clutching an armament-gray Céline bag, surrounded by mostly older men and women in fleece and Tevas. My heart was pounding, and my eyes felt taut with held-in tears. I did the only two things I was capable of in that moment: I kept my butt in the chair, and I paid attention. I noticed that they laughed a lot. I noticed that almost no one mentioned God or any other higher power. I noticed how sad Jerry sounded when he described saying something curt to the young worker trimming his hedges, how he was afraid he'd made the guy fear for his job and regretted it. I wanted to tell Jerry I thought he was being too hard on himself, but I'd also noticed that there was little back-and-forth of that sort. People spoke, and when they were done, they were done, and then we sat until someone else decided to speak. It was like an anthology of monologues, or the Quaker meetings I attended one summer in my twenties in an attempt to find peace of mind and drink less alcohol.

Speaking of alcohol, I noticed that almost no one talked about drinking, or wanting a drink, or how long it had been since they'd had a drink. If you didn't know better, it could have passed as a meeting of just, you know, people with varying levels of manageable problems and conflicts. I got the impression the older men had decades of sober time; as for the others, I couldn't tell. But no one was in crisis. Or, if they were, it wasn't over whether or not to drink. It was over career boredom, or a nagging toothache, or really liking a guy in your dorm who was sending mixed signals. (One of the older guys broke the no-back-and-forth rule at this point, telling the young girl, "Well, I don't think this fellow deserves you!")

I spoke, too. I certainly hadn't planned to. I'm still not sure what made me do it. But in a pocket of silence I just started talking. I barely remember what I said—something about time, something about fear. Something about loving things I used to hate. I know I said The Thing: *Hi, I'm Kristi and I'm an alcoholic.* I'd never said those last three words out loud before. And honestly, I only said them to follow protocol, but as they came out, I knew they were true. I thought it might feel like a weight falling from my shoulders, but it was more like pushing a heavy door open a little wider— wide enough to walk through. When I finished talking, they thanked me and we moved on.

Afterward one of the women gave me a printed meeting schedule and circled some of her favorites. She'd been sober for twenty years and was still hitting five or six meetings a week, she said. Something about that scared me to death and my face must have shown it, because she laughed and said, "It's not from desperation. It's where I see my best friends." Friends, right. I'd almost forgotten what had gotten me through the door. *I need friends. I need friends who know what this is like*, I wanted to tell her, but it suddenly seemed like one confession too many.

"Keep coming back," they said when I left.

"I will," I said. I say a lot of things. Sometimes I mean them and sometimes I don't and sometimes I don't know the difference. That gets better over time, I'm told.

A funny thing happens when you tell people that you've stopped drinking. They say, "Oh, okay." A verbal shrug. Not always, but often enough in my case. Sometimes they say, "Any particular reason why?" and you have the choice of saying, *I just randomly wanted to pull the tablecloth out from under my whole life.* Or, *I just wanted to see if there was still a person in here.* Or, you could be like me and chirp, "Oh, just an experiment for more energy and better sleep!" like someone who makes life plans from *Women's Fitness* magazine. It's an easy path that allows you to keep people at a safe distance, where you can keep an eye on them peripherally, like a paranoid cow.

The week after my AA meeting, someone asked, "Any particular reason why?" and instead of saying, "I just thought it would be fun!" I said, "Just mostly, you know, alcoholism." My heart rate shot up, as if I'd been sprinting, but he laughed in a kind way and said, "Oh, okay, cool."

A few weeks later, I was having dinner with an old friend who asked how long it had taken me to quit drinking once I'd realized I had a problem. "Let's see," I said. "Twelve years, give or take." My friend put down his fork.

"What?" he said. "I've known you almost that long and I had no idea."

I shrugged. "Yeah."

"Well, why didn't you ever tell me?"

"I don't know," I said. "I guess I can tend to be a bit secretive."

He looked at me for a minute while I looked at the tines of his fork, which I thought he might use to stab me. Then he sighed. "Anything else you wanted to reveal? Do you have three children stashed away somewhere? Were you born a dude?"

"That's pretty much it for now," I said.

"Will you tell me if something *else* big happens?"

"Oh, definitely," I said. "Maybe. Probably."

He raised one eyebrow at me, but he also put the fork safely back in his pasta.

"I love you," he said with his mouth half-full. "A lot."

"Thank you," I said. "Same."

Once I pushed that door open, people started walking through. "My mom has twenty years," a woman told me. "I stopped at eighteen," someone said at a cocktail party. A co-worker said, "More than one glass of wine and I feel crappy the whole next day. It's annoying, but I know it's kind of lucky, too."

One acquaintance, the classic too-long-at-the-party guy who could always be counted on to have one more drink, quizzed me closely during a work cocktail function: "Not even socially? Not even wine with dinner? What do you do when everyone else is drinking? Aren't you bored? Seriously, not even on vacation, not even at the holidays, not even on your birthday? What about next time you're in Europe? Or Napa—couldn't you taste and just not swallow?"

I was working up a good mental eye roll. I also knew based on history that we were approaching the ten-minute mark, after which he would give up trying to keep his eyes off my tits. I needed to move them somewhere safe. I made my initial escape noises, at which point he blurted, "Today's my fifth day without a drink."

"Oh!" I said. I didn't want to sound surprised, but the exclamation point inserted itself against my will. "How are you feeling?"

"Okay," he said. "Like a fog is clearing." I nodded. "It's

just hard to imagine not having the occasional celebratory drink," he said. "I'm hoping to eventually become a moderate drinker."

I'd shared that hope once. I'd tried for years to turn myself into a moderate drinker. It turned out adding extra vigilance and stress to a debilitating habit while still utterly failing to drink like a normal person was not the way to go. "It seems like some people are able to do that," I said carefully.

"Do you think you will?" he asked.

"Absolutely not," I said.

"Really? You don't think about just drinking on holidays and shit?"

"Nope."

"But good food is meant to be appreciated with wine," he said. "You don't feel like you're missing out on a big part of life by giving that all up?"

I looked him in the eye. "I made and then broke a promise to myself *every single day* for twelve years," I said. "I failed myself. Every. Single. Day. And now I don't. Do you think I give a fuck whether my *food* could taste 5 percent better?"

He looked miserable. As a vision of the future, I was a letdown. Near us, a group of guys clinked bottles of IPA. I suddenly felt exhausted. It was time to free myself from this situation, go home and kiss my dogs and make out with my husband, or at least kiss my husband and make out with my dogs. "It was nice running into you," I said. "I should be heading home. Congrats on your five days, I know what a big deal that is."

He sighed. "Thanks," he said. "It is. It actually is a really big deal for me. And I just don't know what's going to happen next. I'm pretty scared, to be perfectly honest."

There was still some light in the sky. Through the window, I saw a couple walk away from a bench in the courtyard, leaving it vacant.

"Hey," I said. "I have a little time. Do you want to go sit outside and talk?"

He did.

Desire Lines

Thirty-three days sober, I decide to try eating food outside my house at night again, something I haven't done without alcohol in a decade. John and I go to a neighborhood place that serves hipster updates of stuff our grandparents ate, like oysters Rockefeller and deviled eggs. We've spent countless nights in the reclaimed-wood booths over rye Manhattans, steaks, and big white wines. They know us. In fact, I almost suggested we go someplace new, where no one would register a change. I'm still in the closet as sober. I've only told a few friends, and I feel acutely self-conscious just walking among strangers, as though a sign flashes on me: DO NOT OFFER THIS WOMAN A DRINK. The idea of casual acquaintances knowing something so momentous makes me want to hide in shame. But ultimately, the familiarity and convenience of this place still won out. Our game plan is a simple dinner: no appetizers, no dessert. In and out. "If you're thinking it will be fun, I need you to adjust your expectations downward," I say to John as we're parking the car.

I'm trembling as we sit down in our favorite booth, the round one in the front window. Our usual waitress swings by and says, "Can I start you two off with Manhattans?"

I've already checked the cocktail menu online for something nonalcoholic, but herbal tea and Mexican Coke are the only options. Still, I tilt my head as if I were thinking it over, then say, "Actually, I think just club soda and lime tonight."

"Same here," John says. He won't quit drinking completely for another few months, but he doesn't drink around me, even though I tell him it's okay.

"*Oh*," says our waitress, smiling. "Trying something new!"

I hate her for letting on that she knows anything has changed. I want her to be an entirely different kind of person in an entirely different kind of restaurant who says "Very good, madam" and silently retreats. I'm tempted to blurt "I'm pregnant!" just to stop her from asking, which of course she doesn't. She doesn't know I can't yet tolerate anyone taking an interest in my wobbly new Amish self.

"I might as well have handed her a copy of *The Watchtower*," I say to John when she's gone.

"Oh, come on," he says. He's very relaxed about all of this so I hate him, too. We are witnessing a death and he's too stupid to know it.

"Remember that wedding we went to?" I ask him over our waters.

"Can you be slightly more specific?" he says.

"The one in that no-drinking Baptist church in Ann Arbor where the reception was in the basement and that friend of yours married that guy she'd met in Ireland and then found out he was gay and just wanted a green card and then he vanished and it took forever for the divorce to be official?"

"Oh yeah," John says. "In 1994."

"This is exactly like that wedding."

He's kind enough not to make me walk home.

◻

Thus began the six-month phase of my life characterized primarily by rage at the restaurant industry. I mean, not the entire thing. I made exceptions for restaurants in countries where alcohol was banned, or places I'll likely never visit because they make women walk around in black body bags and can go fuck themselves right off the face of the earth. But the rest of them were directly in my firing line, for the sole reason of lacking fancy enough things for Sober Me to drink.

In my last half a dozen drinking years, I'd become a foodie, prancing all over Seattle eating bone marrow and pickled quince. I ate bagel-and-lox ice cream in New York. I paid a fortune in Florence to eat a pigeon neck stuffed with tripe. In Tokyo, John and I spent two hours combing one block for a no-name, no-sign speakeasy we'd seen in *Gourmet*. We stumbled into a disco, a wrestling gym, and a sushi bar back kitchen before giving up and going to the Park Hyatt like every other *Lost in Translation*–loving tourist in town. My foodieism was partly based on sincere interest but also driven by the fact that I'd started making a lot of money and had picked up the idea from Oprah or some-body that the tasteful thing to spend it on was "experi-ences." For some of my co-workers, this meant taking flying lessons or running marathons in South Africa. I didn't have the risk tolerance for *that* level of adventure, so my experiences often revolved around putting weird and pricey stuff in my mouth. And at that echelon of dining, it's never just about the food; it's about the aperitifs and wines and grappas to go with it, all the drinks crafted or selected with the same obsessive attention to detail and virtually all of them alcoholic. Which was just fine with me, and a handy way to tell myself I was an epicure, not an addict.

In a Munich hotel so modern and stark it had glass-floored elevators, I requested a table for one. "You are eating *alone*?" the host said in exaggerated alarm, hand at his heart.

"Yes," I said, irritated. It was a business hotel, for one thing. Surely I was not the first person to show up for din-ner without a hot piece of ass at my side. I was tired and hungry and flattened out from meeting with depressed col-leagues on depressing topics all day. And, of course, desper-ate for a drink, the part of dinner I always looked forward to most. I gave him a big smile, was rewarded with a window table, and ordered a glass of wine right away.

Wine in hand, I looked at the dinner menu. There were only five entrées, one of them "schnitzel, reinvented." Nor-mally, I would have gone for that because my foodieism had reached such a state that regular *invented* food was no longer enough to fully satisfy me. But a single word in the next entrée threw a wrench in my routine.

"Is this *the* kangaroo?" I asked the waiter. "Or is it some-thing else that's just *called* kangaroo?" He gave me a blank look. "You know, the way mahimahi is called dolphin." An-other blank look. I guess Germans were not all that up on fish trivia.

"It's kangaroo," he said, shrugging.

"I think I have to order that," I said, assuming I had hit on an oddball national staple.

It tasted more or less like venison (and the three glasses of Gewürztraminer I washed it down with weren't the best match). Back home the next week, I asked a German friend, "What's the deal with you guys eating kangaroo?" If you listen closely, you can still hear him laughing.

So yes, I was willing to make an ass of myself over food if it meant something new and shiny to focus my mind and my money on. And especially if it offered cover for my drinking, which it did. Bartenders were making their own syrups and bitters and garnishes from stuff they'd grown on rooftop reclaimed-water gardens, and I wanted to try *all* of it, including one Bloody Mary garnished with house-pickled vegetables and a chunk of locally raised, humanely killed ham. Oh, and flights! I could never pass up the chance to drink four different versions of something under the pretense of studying their nuances. Even the word "flight" promised buoyancy and perspective, though if they'd been called chutes to hell I would have found an upside to that, too.

When I stopped drinking, all my bourbon flights and artisanal gins and biodynamic Chardonnays came to a screeching halt. And so did my pickles and pigeon necks and tender pea shoots harvested by the teeth of fairly paid angels. Because for all the wild creativity at work in Seattle bars, almost none of it was in the service of anything booze-free, and without something sufficiently chic to drink, I couldn't seem to set foot in any of my old foodie haunts. Nonalcoholic drinks were usually limited to club soda and the coffees and teas from the dessert menu, which reminded me of some uber-Christian clients of John's who'd drunk hot chocolate throughout a five-course meal we ate together. The rare mocktail was something sugary and citrus based, more or less a house-made lemonade. One local vegetarian restaurant even offered smoothies as its nonalcoholic options. "A smoothie is a *meal*!" I exclaimed in disbelief, probably a little too loudly. If I didn't want a milk shake, it was Diet Coke ("Chemicals!") or tea ("I'm not drinking *hot liquid* with dinner!") or, the horror, some form of water. If I drank water, how would people know I had taste? How would they know I was cool? How would they know I was anything at all?

Some people say your emotional development stops at whatever age your serious drinking started, and that's where you pick back up when you quit—which would have made me a high school junior in a forty-something body. I don't know how well this theory holds up: my sober self didn't suddenly feel a need to wear Betsey Johnson lace tights and give hand jobs in the backs of cars, much to John's disappointment. Nor did I find myself craving Benson & Hedges Menthol Ultra Lights or poppers. But my teenage self had been desperate to feel like one of the cool kids, and that need reemerged with a startling ferocity that extended to everything I poured down my throat. For me, cool had never meant the most famous scotch or the priciest wine. It was the liquid equivalent of a bowl of steamed baby turnips I'd once cooed over in Seattle's first certified-organic restaurant. Were they good? Sure. Cute? I guess. Were they still a boring root vegetable cooked in the most basic way imaginable? Well, yes. But eating them made me feel noble by association, like one of those people you hear about who can appreciate the simple things in life.

I was not one of those people by a long shot. I was an exhausted, overworked drunk who thought she'd spend the rest of her likely shortened life throwing money at problems she had no other clue how to fix. Eating those turnips let me pretend I was grounded. Paying a lot for them let me feel rich. Sucking down enough booze alongside them let me ignore the fragmented wreck I actually was. And in my pickled mind, it all added up to cool.

I grew up in a mean, new-money, gold-plated Florida town, the municipal equivalent of Trump Tower. We moved there from Georgia the day before I started kindergarten, when my father got a teaching job at the state university. It was a sleepy beach town then, with curving roads designed in World War II to be hard for Nazi invaders to navigate. We spent every weekend in the Atlantic Ocean and most afternoons in the screened-in pool that my dad vacuumed and chlorinated on Sundays. I went to public school and the public library and carried my vinyl dance-shoe tote to a community center that by the looks of it was also designed to be unappealing and unnoticeable to the Nazis.

While we were living our standard professor's-family life, hordes of people began arriving from up north. "Yankees," my parents called them. The word conjured up a jaunty vision that the blunt, demanding people around me didn't exactly match. Why did they talk to waitresses like that? Why did they seem *mad* all the time?

I get it now, kind of. These were city people, used to having to fight to claim their space. They couldn't just turn it off any more than we could turn off being small-town southerners who were shocked when clerks in the city demanded ID with a check. But I was a kid and I couldn't see any of that. I just saw loud and pushy. And rich, based on their cream-colored BMWs, their thick gold necklaces, their popped-collar Ralph Lauren shirts. The tanning parlors they used, when we lived five minutes from the beach. The bottled water they drank, when we all had taps. Their gated communities, with entrances manned by retirees. "They're not even armed," my dad would say. "If someone wants in, what's an old man going to do to stop them?" The school bus ride got a little longer with every gated community we had to enter and exit, and once inside, I'd gawk at the houses with their two-story atriums, like live-in malls.

And their kids. Their mean-as-fuck kids, with their *own* BMWs and gold and popped-collar Polos and insta-tans and hotel room parties. By eighth grade they were pretty much running the world, and my bookish, awkward, middle-class ass with its Mazda-driving parents and house protected only by locks and a cocker spaniel didn't stand a chance. *A dog*, they called me. Or *that*. As in, would you fuck *that*? No, the boys would agree in not-quite-low-enough voices as I stared at my textbook. None of them would fuck *that*. And the fuckable girls would laugh.

Here's where my story could have gone a few different ways. I could have gotten a makeover, become Suddenly Fuckable! Except I actually looked fine—clear complexioned, no more brace-faced than average, tragic perms long in my past. Cute, even. Just, you know, *wrong* in a way that couldn't be fixed at fat camp or the Clinique counter. I could have started handing out sexual favors to convince them I *was so* fuckable, and thank God I didn't do that. Instead, I decided that none of what those mean kids represented— dances, dates, kegs—was something the universe wanted me to have. And then, because somewhere inside I liked myself, I decided that even if I could have that stuff, I didn't want it. Because it was *mainstream*, and mainstream wasn't enough for me.

It was the summer of 1985. I went to the mall and got a short, geometric haircut, with the back shaved like a soldier. I started wearing lace-up black boots and long skirts and red lipstick. I discovered Morrissey and became a primarily cheese-and-Pop-Tart-based vegetarian. In London or New York, I would have just been jumping on a bandwagon, but in South Florida all of this was still fairly new, spread at ground level in record shops and used bookstores. When I returned to school and the boys were extra-super-double grossed out by me, I knew I was onto something good.

There were towns near mine where kids suffered unthinkable privations like inheriting their parents' hand-me-down cars instead of getting a brand-new birthday Porsche, or fighting with their siblings for phone time because the family only had one line. At bookstores and punk clubs, I started to meet those kids and befriend them. I got invited to parties and to hang out at the mall. The more hair I cut off, the prettier people thought I was. Boys (and a few girls) began to declare their affections. Outside my own school and city, I became popular.

Finding a tribe could have softened my attitude toward the kids at school, made me confident enough to slide from culture to subculture and back. I had friends who could pull that off—go to the football game *and* the New Model Army show. But I didn't even try. The rich kids were *mainstream*. Sports—all of them—were *mainstream*. And I rejected all of it before it could reject me. Regular hair-colored hair, tennis shoes, the Sweet Valley High books I'd once devoured. I attended my senior prom, but I did it in quotation marks, in a black column dress and red lips, the Girl Most Likely to Be Mistaken for a Nagel.

My commitment to the path less taken was cemented in college, a tiny enclave of liberal arts, bad behavior, and psychic meltdowns on Florida's Gulf Coast. There was a skeletal core curriculum, but otherwise we designed our courses of study based on whatever our underdeveloped teenage brains found interesting. When I told my adviser I wanted to read all the children's books that had won the Newbery Medal and write a poem in response to each one, or spend a whole semester on George Orwell's travel essays, he didn't bat an eye. I spent four years following the most bewildering path possible to a degree in literature. Given a choice between courses in Shakespeare and Kafka, I picked Kafka. Between Kafka and Gogol, Gogol. I wrote voraciously in unfashionable forms: sestinas, novellas, epistolary poems to a fictional man named Julian, whom I miss. The predominant style among my female classmates was hairy legs and tie-dyes, so I waxed and wore makeup. The music at our parties was parent stuff from the late 1960s, so I went deep into the sort of proto-twee U.K. bands who wrote songs about Yuri Gagarin and Eva Marie Saint.

My fixation on staying off any path that looked walkable also meant finding wonderful secret music and books and films wherever I looked. Because I *had* to look or be culture-free. I started to see that there was art and food and even colors to match not just the big emotions like love and grief but their small adjacencies. I became an expert at recognizing odd-shaped emotions, and accessorizing them, and finding the talismans to evoke them. A curator of my own life. This is where the world opened up and also where my future troubles began.

Soon after graduation I saw the Louis Malle film *Damage*, in which the married British politician Jeremy Irons has an obsessive affair with his own son's fiancée, played by Juliette Binoche. At the end, having ruined pretty much everything ruinable in every character's life, Jeremy is living in self-exile in a bare, whitewashed flat in a Mediterranean town.

The last shot pulls back to show him sitting penitent in a hard wooden chair in front of a wall-sized blowup of a photograph taken of himself, his son, and Juliette, just before all the lying and hiding and fucking on hard marble floors and untimely deaths began.

It's meant to be a chilling conclusion, and it is. But for me it was also a kind of curation porn. The leather sandals on his feet, the single apple and wedge of cheese on a plate, the curtainless window and bleached wood floor. Only Louis Malle could make exile look so chic. But the simplicity also called to me—the notion that the objects around us could signify who we were, especially if we wiped the slate clean first. I thought about the core objects I carried from apartment to apartment. A postcard from a boy I'd loved but hadn't seen in years, inscribed with lines from a Billy Bragg song. The woven coin purse a friend brought me from her home in Caracas, with a few centimos inside for luck. The Swiss Army Knife I'd bought in Switzerland thinking it wasn't sold anywhere else in the world. I thought that these objects together gave me some sense of who I was, though I couldn't have put it into words. Which didn't stop me from trying. For the next several years, I tried to write a story about a woman who sold everything she owned and started over in a single room. I never got very far, because I couldn't figure out what objects she would put in that room, because I had no idea who she was. But there was some satisfaction in starting her story over and over and over again, thinking each time was the time I'd get it right.

•

I spent the months after that first sober dinner out making
ever-more-troublesome mocktails at home: zesting Meyer
lemons, boiling sage leaves into syrup, chopping pineapple
for *agua fresca*. But at some point my Mocktail Fever had
to break, if only because it was so much work. Soda with a
few drops of bitters—and maybe a squeeze of lime if I could
be bothered to slice one—became my new norm. John
stopped drinking six months after I did, and maybe he
was just trying to spare us a second round of lunacy, but
he was much calmer about restaurants than I was. One
night at Mamnoon, a sleek Middle Eastern place in a
hipster-dense part of Seattle, he said to our waiter, "Can
you ask the bartender to make me something nonalcoholic
that isn't sweet?"

I stared wide-eyed at him. "You just *asked* for that."

John shrugged. "We'll see what I get." What he got
was a coupe glass filled with something that tasted a little
like tea, a little like soda, and a lot like belonging. It was
delicious.

Sometimes I try those same words in the same casual
tone, but the results aren't as thrilling. I'm more likely to
say, "I'm fine with water," and mean it. Because I just don't
really care what the liquid in my glass says about me anymore. I'd like to tell you it's because sobriety cured my need
for specialness. I'd also like to tell you I invented the stapler
and can start fires with my mind. But no.

In some ways I became one of those kids from my hometown. I know how to have money and spend it. I can pass
without visible effort in the world of mainstream luxury
and "belong." But I still hate those crass little fucks and

everyone who reminds me of them. And I'm convinced they see through my veneer of belonging to the awkward, unsexy, merely middle-class kid inside. So I skirt the edges, camouflaging myself with baby turnips and bleak movies so no one can spot me and kick me back out of the club I'm not sure I wanted to join in the first place.

At this moment I'm drinking a coffee I chose because the café chalkboard said it had "notes of marionberry" and I love weird berries. The coffee was made with an AeroPress, the most low-tech way imaginable to make a five-dollar cup. When I first excitedly described AeroPress coffee to John, he stared blankly at me and then said, "That's camping coffee. You won't even sleep in a hotel without room service and you're going around drinking camping coffee?"

I'm wearing plain black flats that look like all the other plain black flats in the world, but these are from *Belgium*. In the last twenty-four hours I've said of a film, "It's a B movie, but in the *exact right way*." I've made an argument for "Hairshirt" being the best R.E.M. song. I've purchased a mascara in the shade Too Black, just to see if it was true (it's not). Sobriety didn't end my love for the road less traveled. How could it? It *is* the road less traveled. And once you're already on that road, the side paths look more like trampled vegetation than anything officially sanctioned. Land planners call them desire lines, which is a kind way to say *The places we didn't think it made any goddamn sense to walk*. That's where you can find me, if you want. And if you don't want, that's fine, too. I don't really want to hang out with you anyway.

The Barn

"You realize everyone thinks we're a couple," Mindy says as we leave the Airfield Estates tasting room. "Because you keep saying 'we.' 'We love Viognier!' "

"We *do* both love Viognier," I say. "I'm using the English language with efficiency and precision." Mindy unlocks her SUV, and we each hoist a case of wine into the back. It's over a hundred degrees out, and I have the unscientific thought that the compressed heat in the car could actually shatter the bottles.

She shuts the hatch. "I'm just making you aware that we sound like lesbian life partners."

"A lot of women would be proud to have me on their arm," I say. We turn back to face the strip mall of tasting rooms we'd just come from. "Dusted Valley next?"

At Dusted Valley the pourer offers Viognier right away. "I love Viognier!" I say, and wave a hand at Mindy. "I don't know what this person likes."

I love the taste of wine, but I hate wine tasting. For one thing, even though I'm a diligent spitter-not-swallower, it still gets me a little buzzed, and I have no interest in being anything other than a *lot* buzzed. But I also don't want to be like those tasters who spill out of limos, all red-faced and loud and looking like the kinds of people who use "hot tub" as a verb. So I'm stuck being me—someone who pretends to like sipping tiny amounts of wine, when really she wants to hunker down, alone, with a bottle.

I hardly ever know what to say about the wine. Generally, my evaluation is that it tastes, you know, good. If the pourer looks expectant, sometimes I'll grab onto a word from the tasting notes. "Oh, yes, granite!" I try hard to appreciate the subtleties. I want to, desperately. If I learn to experience the whole world of wine in one sip, maybe that will be enough. Maybe I won't finish the whole first bottle, crack a second, and stumble to bed ashamed. Again.

Mindy and I are only on this romantic wine jaunt because of a shared refusal to take a predawn plane ride for a day of corporate training. She's a fearful flier who only sucks it up for better destinations than Kennewick, Washington, and I have a blanket policy against getting to Sea-Tac by 5:00 a.m. for a thirty-minute flight. It is a four-hour drive from Seattle to Kennewick, which allows us to leave at a civilized hour and pass through wine country on our way home.

The Washington climate changes dramatically on the eastern side of the Cascades. It's much hotter in the summer, with stretches that look like desert. "Except for almost everything, we could be Thelma and Louise," I remark around Ellensburg as I watch tumbleweeds bounce by.

"Corporate Drone Thelma and Louise," Mindy says.

We didn't always feel like drones. When we met six years ago, we were raring to go, the kind of people who would hop on 5:00 a.m. flights without question if that's what the company asked us to do. I was direct from the Midwest then and lurching around Seattle like a lost dog. My jeans were too baggy, my shoes too flat, my phone too unsmart. My office building was seventy-six floors high, and I got disoriented just navigating the various elevator banks to get to meetings. "I spend my days riding around in a series of tubes," I said in an e-mail to my former boss in Michigan, hoping he would beg me to come back.

I was overwhelmed and barely able to contain my panic. I was responsible for three times as many people as I had been, with a much broader scope of work, yet there was no training or orientation, and I had maybe thirty minutes a week with my boss, at most. Mindy and I reported to the same vice president, whose jolly-midwesterner persona hid a tendency to turn on people fast and hard. The way he could rain praise on me one day and make dark comments about my future the next slammed me right back to childhood.

Mindy terrified me, too, by being beautiful, math fluent, and preternaturally calm in an environment so pressured I'd seen people's hands shake in meetings. One day she invited me to coffee, and after a few minutes of small talk I hesitantly confessed my sense of full-spectrum wrongness.

"We all feel like that," she said. "This place feeds on fear. It has nothing to do with you."

The relief of realizing it wasn't just me allowed me to temporarily overlook the fact that my new employer was notorious for *feeding on people*. I internalized it soon enough, though. It wasn't that the people I worked with were mean (except for my boss, that is, when his Mr.-Hyde-in-Dockers side came out). It's just that the scope of the company's ambitions far outstripped the resources available to achieve them, and that was mostly on purpose. It was assumed that each employee could do the work of two or three people via "ruthless prioritizing" or "smart trade-offs" or other rational-sounding methods that in reality panned out more as working through weekends and answering e-mails at midnight knowing you'd wake up at 6:00 a.m. to a flood of new ones. It was possible to hold it together for a while if you were young and adrenalized with ambition, or if the only person in your life to let down was you. But as people got older (for example, over thirty) and especially as they started families, some of them looked around, decided that feeding themselves into a meat grinder every day was no longer bearable, and hit the road. Women left in especially large numbers, sometimes to stay home and raise kids but more often, in my experience, for other companies. And those of us who stayed got used to being the Only Woman at the Table.

Being the Only Woman at the Table means spending a lot of time trying to talk, because there are mere microseconds between one man finishing his thought and the next one jumping in and no one bothers to read nonverbal cues, or talking and seeing half the room choose that moment to look at their phones. It means being interrupted over and over until you either give up or resort to saying "Can I please finish my thought?" like a prig who can't just roll with the discussion. Or, finally expressing a whole thought and having the conversation pick back up as though you hadn't said a word. It means that no one will meet your eye, how could they when they're too busy staring each other down, and if they do, it's with an irritated blankness; they aren't listening, just waiting for you to stop talking so they can start again, the way a table of adults will humor a child tediously recounting a Pixar plot. And this is what it's like with the *good* guys. Most of the men I worked with were good guys who knew intellectually that women deserved to be at the table and be heard, even if they couldn't get their lizard brains to play along.

Sometimes the good guys around me seemed to feel odd or even guilty about the dramatic imbalance in our numbers. Mindy and I once constituted the female 8 percent of a corporate retreat group where, during introductions, many of the men took pains to mention their wives. "I run Consumables for Europe," one man said. "But the real boss is my wife, who manages me and our kids." Or, "I'm general counsel for North American retail. My wife is also a former lawyer who promoted herself to CEO of our household when the kids were born." Mindy and I had avoided sitting together, lest we be seen as a massive, threatening bloc of femaleness. Now we swapped glances across the conference table as man after man explained how his work paled in comparison to that of his smarter, stronger, kinder, more organized better half. It was hard not to wonder if this was some corporate Kabuki they were putting on for us.

After dinner, Mindy and I head back to our motel in nearby Prosser and then decide to go out for a drink, which is when we realize that Prosser is a daylight town. Everything along Wine Country Road is closed except for one big red building set back from the road.

"It looks like a barn," I say.

"It's called the Barn," Mindy says. We look at each other, shrug, and pull into the parking lot just as the Barn's shuttle van is pulling out.

"Oh goody, a bar with its own shuttle bus," I say, because my standards involve driving drunk in my own car, very carefully.

It doesn't smell like a barn, though it does smell like wet carpet and frying oil, and the only thing in the lobby is a busted ATM that you can tell has been that way for a while. We walk down a short hallway into the bar, or perhaps it's the set of *The Accused*. The room is full of men, and every single one of them stops talking and turns to look at us. "Jesus," I say under my breath. But Mindy and I are genetically coded by now to not run from rooms full of men. And there's two of us. And we want a drink. There are two seats open at the bar, and we take them while the men stare as though their space has been invaded by antelope on pogo sticks. I nod at the two on my left, gray-haired guys still in their reflective construction vests, and they nod back. "Ladies," one says.

Now that we've claimed space, I survey whatever I can
without turning my head and being obvious about it. It's
just a bar, with signs for low-end beers and rolls of shiny
lottery tickets and no windows (but also no stripper poles).
Dim lighting, Toto on the jukebox, vinyl seats patched with
tape. What I think of with no self-awareness whatsoever as
a Drinker's Bar. The kind of place you go specifically to get
drunk. The kind of place I never go, because I don't con-
sider myself someone who ever *sets out* to get drunk; I am
someone who sets out to enjoy a glass of wine or two, and
then things sort of snowball from there. We order some
local Pinot Gris (in wine country, even Drinker's Bars have
good wine lists) and relax a bit as the men absorb the dis-
turbance in their field and return to their conversations.

Most of them do, anyway. The man next to Mindy leans
over and says, "Y'all sisters?" He looks like a younger but
much more weathered Kris Kristofferson.

"No, we're not sisters," Mindy says. Other than both
being dark-haired human women, Mindy and I don't look
anything alike. I'm tempted to ask if all the men in the bar
are brothers.

"Leave them alone, Carl," says the guy next to me.
"Don't mind him. He's harmless."

"It's fine," I say. Carl has put his head down sideways on
the bar and is staring at Mindy. I raise an eyebrow at her to
say, *Do you want to go?*

"It's fine," she says. So we stay and gradually get into
normal bar chat with the guy next to me and his friends.
"Y'all aren't from around here, are you?" he asks. No, we tell
him, we're from Seattle, in town for work. The men also

work nearby, mostly in logging, and live in the RV park behind the bar.

"I can show you my trailer," Carl offers.

One of my tricks for steering a conversation away from whether I want to see someone's trailer is to become deeply interested in its least sexy details. To that end, over two more glasses of wine I pummel the men around us with questions about their specific logging jobs, the logging industry in general, Prosser, and the rest of the Yakima valley. And they seem to like it, or at least they give me real answers. Maybe it's a novelty having a woman want to know so much about them. I'm about to delve into the types of trees they cut down when I notice Mindy staring over my shoulder.

I turn to see Carl, standing by a barrel-shaped cooler of beer with his T-shirt pulled up. He's grabbed two handfuls of ice and is rubbing them on his nipples while grinning at us and doing some sort of hula.

I drop my investigative-reporter act. "What the fuck," I say.

The man next to me shrugs apologetically. "Try to take it as a compliment," he says.

I've been advised to take a lot of strange behavior as a compliment. When a boy shoved me on the playground, it meant he liked me. When guys dumped me, it meant they knew I was way too good for them. When men talk over me in meetings, it's because they're threatened by my intellect; when they catcall me in the park, it's because I've still got it. I've been surfing a wave of male aggression all my life. But the nipple icing was a new one.

"We should probably head out," I say to Mindy. *No, no!* the other men protest. *Ignore Carl. Just one more round, on us.*

Well, in that case.

That's the thing about this bar: no one will bat an eye at how much I drink. No one will want to leave before I do, or switch to soda because they've got an early meeting tomorrow. They'll go as long as I do, or longer. It thrills and scares me, just as it thrills and scares me to be getting drunk with a bunch of men I don't know. These men don't hide or apologize for their drinking, and they don't expect me to, either. In those other rooms full of men, I am always polished and on guard: just female enough to be unthreatening, just male enough to be visible. Here, I could get sloppy if I wanted to: drink from the bottle, commandeer the jukebox, throw up. Maybe the most chivalrous man in the bar would try to sober me up with black coffee at some point, or maybe the creepiest would try to take me to his RV. But no one would think, *Now there's a chick who needs to get her life together.*

It's the main reason that I avoid Drinker's Bars: I don't know how far I'd fall if I didn't have to fake being a normal drinker. If I could toss my list of rules and just disappear into the windowless box full of lotto tickets and well brands and idle chatter and brain fog. I can't risk it. I need to pretend that my drinking is an accompaniment to the *real* event: catching up with a friend, or networking with colleagues, or eating dinner with my husband. I need the tropes of alcohol as an artisanal passion around me to keep me in line. I need someone waiting for me to say, "Yes, I do

taste notes of plum and dirt," or to praise the lemon ver-
bena syrup sourced from the bar's own living rooftop. Take
away my money or my extreme whiteness, and it might be
clear that getting a lot of ethanol into my bloodstream as
fast as possible is all I really care about. I could be a whole
different kind of drunk.

Instead, I'm the kind who turns this bar into an anecdote. Mindy and I stay for one more round, wake up a little
hungover the next morning, and go wine tasting in her new
Lexus, laughing about the Barn and Carl and his nipples
in between stops. In Seattle we return to our rooms full of
men, those high-earning, high-fiving guys. "It's nice to be
back to civilization," I tell one of them when he asks about
our trip, and I slide into my seat at the conference table,
dressed up, laptop open, already dreaming of that evening's
glass or two of cold white wine that will become a whole
bottle at room temperature. It will take years for me to see
that civilization was not where I belonged then. The Barn
was my rightful home, and those men were my brothers.

How to Be a Moderate Drinker

1. Only drink on certain days of the week.

Only on weekends, or only on weekdays, or only on every other day. Make sure that on the nondrinking days you think of nothing else but drinking.

2. Decide in advance how many drinks you will have, and once you've had that many, stop.

Two is a good number. After two drinks your prefrontal cortex will be in the perfect state to make wise and unfun choices.

3. A standard drink is five ounces. Measure your drinks so you don't accidentally have too much.

If five ounces looks too sad, pour both of your five-ounce drinks into one glass. Then forget that counted as two drinks and pour another ten ounces. Then have as many more drinks as you want of whatever size you want.

4. Drink a glass of water between each glass of wine to cut down on the buzz and keep you hydrated.

Or just sort of nurse one glass of water all night and call it good. Wine is basically water, anyway.

5. Write down every drink in a notebook, to stay accountable and observe your habits over time.

Note the date, time, and amount of each drink. Get specific about varietal and region. Note flavors and mouthfeels, who you were with, what you were wearing. Let it be erotic fan fiction.

6. Make a habit of socializing with nondrinkers.

Totally. Just use Google Maps to find the nearest tabernacle and show up with your Scrabble board. Try not to let them see your hands shaking over the tiles.

7. Drink only things you don't like.

Sure. Switch to red. Switch to tequila. Guess what? You'll learn to love what you hate and they'll still drop a veil over you.

8. Stop drinking as soon as you feel buzzed.

Good idea! Also stop eating when your food tastes too good. Stop having sex when you think you might come. Stop the movie before the finale.

9. Don't drink when you are sad, anxious, or lonely.

That's funny.

10. Practice mindful drinking. Savor each sip. When you want more, first ask yourself, "What need is this drink fulfilling?" When the need is filled, just stop.

Yes. Good idea. What need is this drink serving? Or this one. Or maybe just one more. Is panic a need? Is horror? What if my needs have blood-drawing teeth? Should I just pause to name these needs for you while they chew my skin and spit it out? Help me, please. I want to do this right.

Pussy Triptych

I'm eighteen, drunk, and about to fuck a boy at a party. I'm not that into him, but he's been hanging around for weeks, and I've set a goal to sleep with at least three guys by September so I can start college knowing everything there is to know about sex.

We make out a little, and then he pushes my Fiorucci dress up around my waist and unzips his jeans. I'm not even wet yet, but I don't want to come across as, you know, *needy*. He pushes me down on all fours—a first for me, but okay—and tries to put it where I wasn't expecting him to.

"Wrong hole," I say. He laughs and ignores me.

"Stop it," I say. "I'm serious."

"C'mon," he says, still poking around. "It won't hurt."

"*I said stop.*"

"Okay, calm down," he says.

Now would be a good time for me to get up and leave, except he's already course corrected and is inside me. I no longer want him there, but okay. Soon, very soon, we're done.

"I didn't realize you were so *conservative*," he says as I pull my dress down.

"Try asking first next time," I say, while thinking, *Am I too conservative?* We leave the pool house and he goes back to the party and I never see him again. (Turns out he was sent to military school a few weeks later.) I join my girl-friends under a sea grape tree. "You guys," I say, "Eric just tried to *buttfuck* me. *Twice.*"

We howl with laughter. Someone passes a plastic jug of vodka, and we toast to the occasion. Something inside me is quivering like a scared animal, but the cheers and vodka cover it up, and I'm just a cool, emancipated chick laugh-ing with her friends after fending off unwanted anal sex.

I'd like to say this was the last time I confused pickled self-destruction with emancipation, but I was just getting started.

I got a music journalist ten years my senior to visit me from New York, and I seduced him fifty feet from where my parents were sleeping. I fucked a guy from France in the deep end of a pool five minutes after he told me I was nothing special to look at. I slept with a diplomat's son who never looked at me again, and turned down a shaggy, skinny poet because he looked at me so kindly. I got a stoner off with my foot through his jeans while six people slept around us. I permanently scarred my elbow having sex in an awkwardly shaped bathtub. I got HPV and had my cervix frozen to kill precancerous cells, twice. I fell in love with a man from Vermont and took him back over and over when he cheated over and over, even when he put his hands on other women right in front of me.

I drove drunk to meet up with men instead of taking taxis because calling a taxi would be admitting I was making drunk sex plans. I never had an accident, but I forgot where I parked sometimes. And on Halloween 1991 I ran over a black cat.

I told men I'd come when I hadn't, because it wasn't their fault I was too drunk to feel anything. I lied about what I liked and didn't like in bed to accommodate whomever I was in bed with. If I liked something I thought I shouldn't, I lied about that, too. I lied to wretched men and wonderful men. When I finally met the one who lit me up through the alcohol haze, who knew exactly how to crack me up and kiss me and love me, I was so scared he'd leave that I spent years trying to make it so. The night before our wedding, I set my hair on fire trying to light a cigarette.

I told secrets to strangers. I told other people's secrets to strangers. From time to time I'd make up a secret to tell to strangers, just because. And all the while, as my world grew smaller and darker and more brittle, I told myself, *This is freedom.*

□

I'm forty-three and it's my last year drinking. I'm in Frankfurt for work, staying in a chilly, artsy hotel that reminds me of old *SNL* "Sprockets" sketches. Tomorrow is Sunday, my jet-lag recovery day before the workweek starts. Around 9:00 p.m., I decide to go to the bar for one glass of wine. Just one. I'll drink it slowly. I even bring a book to focus my attention.

The bar has a dark, cozy vibe out of step with the Brutalist feel of the rest of the place, and the bartender is olive-skinned with a gleaming smile. I drink my one glass of Gewürztraminer, then another. (This isn't breaking my promise to myself; when I say one, I always mean two.) I read my book slowly and chat with an older couple from New York. The bartender fills my glass a third time. "Oh, I'm fine," I say, but he smiles and says it's on him. "To welcome the beautiful American to Germany," he says. "The night is young."

The night is *not* young, and I'm dehydrated and sallow from the flight, not beautiful. But I am also a paranoid American, convinced that every European who meets me sees only the simian smirk of George W. Bush, and it makes me overly susceptible to the kindness of strangers. Even if that stranger is paid to be kind. I raise my glass to him. "Danke," I say. He winks.

The room is thinning out when a stunning, Slavic-looking blonde in a fur coat sweeps in and takes the stool next to me. The bartender greets her by name—Basia—and hands over a glass of amaretto. She is simply, impeccably turned out—black dress, heels, diamond studs, full makeup. Next to her, I feel like Mary Ann from *Gilligan's Island*. She lights a cigarette—she even looks good smoking—and comments on my book. I forgot about the book at least one drink ago, but I rally and we talk about the series, by an Italian woman who writes under a pseudonym, which she is also reading.

"Without anonymity she would not feel free to tell what she does," Basia says.

"That may be true, but it's a shame. Women shouldn't have to hide themselves to tell the truth."

She shrugs the most European shrug of all time. "This will not change," she says. The bartender, returning from a booth across the room, leans between us and refills my glass, squeezing my shoulder as he does.

I should probably find that odd. I do, a little. But why worry? I'm a smart woman, a master traveler, used to drinking alone in foreign countries. And I'm not even alone now that the glamorous, learned Basia has befriended me. I am proving my worthiness to be here with the cultured people of the world. My bed is an elevator ride away, and if I'm a little worse for wear tomorrow morning, a big German breakfast will set things right.

We drink and talk some more—I drink—Basia is still working on that one small amaretto. The bartender keeps topping off my glass, and I lose track of how much I've had. At one point he pours one for himself and leans across the bar to talk to me. Where am I from? How long will I be in town? He is unabashedly flirting, which strikes me as funny—he's at least ten years younger than I am. But that's what men do. They flirt. And a woman like me watches, wryly amused and a little flattered, then pays the check and walks coolly away, to wake raccoon-eyed but alone.

It's after midnight when Basia gets a text. "Time to go," she says. "Come with me. I'll walk you to your room."

The bartender protests. "We are open two more hours! Don't leave me," he says to me. "Stay and talk. The night is still young." The night is apparently always young with this guy.

Basia's eyes suddenly flash with something dangerous

and she speaks in German to him and he says something back with a sneer. "Come," she says again. I slide off the bar stool and once my feet hit the carpet, I realize how drunk I am. Don't let it show, I order myself—as if I were still in control, as if I could convince anyone that a bottle and a half of wine (at least) didn't put a dent in me—and I pull my muscles inward to hug my bones.

"Gute Nacht," I tell the bartender. He gives me a small, tight smile. Maybe I'm not beautiful anymore. I've seen it happen before.

Basia walks me to the elevator. "You have your key?" she says. I nod. "I couldn't leave you with him," she says. "He's not safe with women. You would be sorry."

"Oh, I'd be fine," I say breezily, or maybe it's my body that's swaying breezily.

She stares at me. "He hurt my friend," she says. "You would not be fine."

In the elevator we punch different floors. Hers is first. "So you are staying here, too?" I ask, wanting to bring the conversation back to glam-woman topics. "My client is," she says, and her eyes narrow. "You do realize I'm an escort?"

"Yes," I say. "Of course." I can't tell if she believes me or not.

I enter my room giggling, congratulating myself on a night of adventure: good white wine in a chic European bar, book talk with the world's most glamorous prostitute, and the defeat of an ill-intentioned man. *You'll remember this night forever*, I think. Before I pass out, I go through the motions of washing my face, brushing my teeth, and drinking a glass of water—hangover prevention. It's important to me that I do all the things an actual drunk would forget to do.

I wake under the white duvet, unable to turn my head without zags of pain. My eyes feel parboiled. I lie on my side staring at the windowsill. *A prostitute saved you from being raped in a foreign country*, I think. *And no one would have believed you. You'd just be some married woman who fucked a hot young bartender and tried to blame him for it. A hooker took care of you because you can't take care of yourself.* I push myself upright and sit naked and cross-legged on the bed. *Remember this night*, I tell myself. *Remember this forever.*

Eventually, I force myself off the bed, pull on the same jeans and boots I left on the floor last night, and take the elevator downstairs, going out of my way to say a cheerful "Guten Tag!" to all the people I see so they will understand that I am a healthy and successful person. I turn left outside the hotel and walk for two miles, stopping at a Turkish restaurant when my head has cleared and I'm finally hungry. Only "cleared" for me is more like "erased." The events of the night before are rewriting themselves into a minor anecdote. I had a little too much to drink and got into a bit of a scrape. On the walk back, I feel almost cheerful. *Just watch yourself a little better, kiddo.*

But something must have stuck around, because I don't go back to the bar that night. And I only drink one bottle of wine, alone in my room.

▣

I'm forty-six, sober, and traveling back in time just long enough to leave a note for my teenage self to find after the thwarted buttfucking:

Hey. Nice save back there. Personally, I wouldn't have let him fuck me after what he tried to pull. But your body, your choice and all that.

Look. I need you to know that this kind of stuff will keep happening. The world of teenage boys and the world of men are a lot alike, it turns out. Men will keep trying to ignore whatever limits you set. I don't know why. Maybe they had lousy fathers, maybe they think "no" means "convince me," maybe they're just desperate for whatever bits of power they can grab. The whys aren't the point. The point is, you don't have to make it so easy for them to hurt you. You think that shrugging off their aggression is a show of power. You think that matching them drink for drink and then blowing them in their cars makes you cool. But making a choice when you're too drunk to think of anything else to do is giving your power away. Give your body away if you want, but not your power. And not your judgment. You're going to need both.

You think sexual freedom is your birthright and that no one should tell you how to use your body. You're right, but it doesn't matter. You know how the creepy old bagger at Publix always tells you to smile and it drives you nuts? Men will still be doing that in your forties. Remember in sixth grade when that boy cornered you in the hall and grabbed your crotch and the first thing the principal said when you reported it was "Did you have a hall pass?" That'll stick with you, and in twenty-five years when a man walks up and grabs your breast when you're just walking down a street in Paris, you won't report it. You'll tell yourself it's because reporting a crime in a foreign city will just give him even more of your time and energy, but deep down you know it's because talking to the gendarmes would be humiliating. After all, you weren't even raped, *you will tell yourself.*

This shit is happening around you right now, more than you know. In the last few years, scores of women have accused Bill Cosby of rape, starting from before you were born. He might be raping someone right this second in your time, or mine, or both. But despite the accusations from women of all ages and geographies, a lot of people think it's all just a big conspiracy. It's easier for them to believe that a bunch of women would band together to ruin Bill Cosby's life for fun and profit than it is for them to believe that maybe, just maybe, Cliff Huxtable is a rapist.

That's what it's like out here in your future.

Oh, and then there's the president of the United States. (You already know his name, but I'm not going to tell you who he is because you would never in a quintillion fucking years believe me.) During the campaign, he was caught bragging on tape that he gets away with grabbing women's pussies uninvited because he's famous. And it sent the country into an uproar. Even men! Men got mad about sexual assault. *It was a beautiful moment.*

Then he won the election.

He won because when it came right down to it, people didn't really care what he did to women. Not that America doesn't love its women. Who wouldn't love those soft, pretty creatures so willing to be sacrificed over and over? Who wouldn't love those patient, selfless dumb fucks?

Believe me, that's not the kind of love you want. So don't sacrifice yourself. Don't roll over. Don't trust in good intentions. Don't think you're too special to be hurt. Don't blunt your own brain.

Save yourself and save me, too.

P.S.: And stop calling yourself fat. You're not. *Jesus Christ.*

Useful

It was raining steadily, making the entire Washington State Fair an electrocution opportunity. John and I stumbled off the Tilt-A-Whirl and into the nearest exhibition barn, where I spotted some blue-ribbon Katahdin sheep. "Oh, I have four of those!" I said.

"I'm sorry, what?" John said.

"Katahdin sheep. I have four. In *FarmVille*."

"Ah. Thank you for clarifying."

Seems as if John should have remembered what an accomplished and sensibly diversified fake farmer I was. But in his defense, my mental faculties can be a bit . . . unpredictable in intense weather. Heat in particular brings out a bedazzled aphasia in me. On a trip to Florida, on a day that topped out at 103, I announced that an elevator we were in had "European-style seating." I caught my mistake. "Flooring. European-style flooring." John raised his eyebrows. "You know what I mean," I said. "The ground floor says *G*, not 1. The first floor is the first floor!"

The elevator door opened. "And now we are at *our* floor,"

John said, "where we are going to get you into some air-conditioning before things get any worse."

Later that day, we took a walk on the beach and I spotted a little kid fishing in the ocean. "Look at that boy shopping out there!" I told John. "So cute."

"It is amazing that you grew up here and survived," he said.

Jet lag could also set me off. "I can't find the switches for the upper brightness," I'd once lamented in an Italian hotel room. But that day at the fair I was simply stating facts. I *did* have four Katahdin sheep that each produced four milks and two fertilizers per feeding, making them highly valuable to my farm and especially its yogurt operation.

I had *FarmVille*'d my ass off in the two months I'd been sober. When the 9:00 p.m. jitters hit, I planted wheat. When I left a stressful meeting thinking, *God, I can't wait to have a glass of wine*, and then remembered I didn't drink anymore, I'd duck into my office and collect eggs. On my tenth day without a drink, when John and I had a dumb spat about how to cope with an incompetent mortgage refinance rep (I wanted to just get it done, while John felt we should bury his body under the plum tree and start over), it hit me that I was stuck in a perfect drinking situation and couldn't drink. And my life would continue to be harder and conflict-ridden as a result, though perhaps less so after my inevitable divorce. Deep breathing did fuck-all to calm me down, but rearranging my fake plots to cluster the berries and flowers together made the night manageable, and one more manageable night was a win.

I didn't talk much about my significant *FarmVille* accomplishments to anyone but John. "It's not *real*," a co-worker once said when I mentioned it.

"Sure it is," I said. "It's *really* moving pixels around a screen."

"But don't you feel like it's just an escape from life?" he pressed.

"Yes, I do," I said, and maybe I said it in a scary way, because he let it drop, which saved me from having to mention his fantasy football league. Look, I admire people who can spend all their time living smack in the middle of their problems and fears. But if I had that innate capability, I probably wouldn't have become a drunk. And in early sobriety I saw nothing wrong with taking my reality in small doses.

And the sheep at the Washington State Fair *were* real. Their wool was dense and humid. They smelled like sheep murk, not pixels. I was absolutely thrilled to meet them, and the square-pupiled goats, and the rabbits that, let's face it, don't seem to bring a lot to the party other than fluff. "Look," I said to John. "It's those chickens with little feather Village People pants!" "Look, this cow is making intense eye contact with me!" "Look, this bunny has cow spots—it's a Holstein rabbit!"

And this was before we'd even gotten to the hall with the gourds and prize vegetables. This was real farming—real *life*, full of nonalcoholic wonder—and I wanted to see everything, everything.

Normally, I would have spent June through August drinking wine al fresco. But I'd canceled Rosé Season for myself just as it was getting started, so I had to fall back on the lesser-known season, Summer.

Summer in Seattle is an experience of collective hypomania, three months when the entire city tries to cram in as much activity as possible before the light disappears again. Our daylight, which ends by 4:00 p.m. in December, stretches until after 10:00 in July. The mist dries up, and the temperature rises to our upper-tolerable limit of seventy-seven degrees. Like nineteenth-century Austrians, we take the air to cure ourselves of the damage seasonal affective disorder has done to our minds and hearts. Summer in Seattle brings outdoor Shakespeare, kayaking, paddleboard yoga. There is a festival where people sleep in tents just to hear Dave Matthews Band play their four-hour songs. "Dave Matthews!!!!!!!!" they post to Facebook.

Once I quit drinking and actually had energy to spend, I threw myself into square and wholesome things. On Saturdays I'd come home from the farmers' market and spread all my loot out on the kitchen counter. "Isn't it interesting that carrots can be vastly different colors, but taste the same?" I asked John. "Or do you think there are subtle taste variances that a carrot expert would pick up on right away?"

"Carrot expert?" he said.

"There's not a thing in this world that doesn't have its own expert," I told him.

I made pesto out of kale and sorrel and everything else I could think of that wasn't plain old basil (though I made plenty of basil pesto, too). I wandered the aisles of garden stores, smelling pineapple sage and chocolate mint. I filled the backseat of my car with dahlias, planted them in a raised bed, and made short, densely packed bouquets like the ones I'd seen in *Martha Stewart Living*. I dragged John to parks and petting farms. I thought I was just coming back to life, but one day, watching me bottle-feed a baby goat, John said, "You're trying to become Useful again, aren't you?" and I realized yes, I was doing that, too.

John and I had tried to become Useful together once, by moving to a farm. Well, to what used to be a farm. A daffodil farm. Okay, we were not the Joads. But we were in earnest. We lasted a year.

We were in our twenties, not yet married, and living the postgrad life in Ann Arbor. We had spent our school years studying literature and art history and philosophy and emerged not knowing what to do with any of it. We had for-now jobs that paid the bills and gave us places to go every morning, but that was just until we got a foothold in the world doing . . . something. We might have been privileged and naive, but we were serious about finding our purpose, and finding it in the Midwest, which felt exotically solid and American. Nothing like our South Florida childhoods, full of banana trees and wild parakeets and winter trips to the waterslide park, but no ice-skating or snowball fights or cozy nights in front of glowing hearths— no roaring fires at all except for the ones that periodically burned in the Everglades. We had no *history*; nearly everything was new in South Florida, including the people, who arrived for the winter from up north, or forever from Cuba, coming by the tens of thousands in the Mariel boatlift. I was nineteen before I ever went north of the Mason-Dixon Line and thought the thirty-five-degree Christmases at my grandparents' house in Alabama were almost unfathomably cold.

To my young eyes, it also seemed as if no one in South Florida really *did* anything. Not anything tangible, anyway. Or Useful. At least not in my affluent white town, where all the men worked in offices and their wives stayed home. Retirees made up much of the population, and their main activities were shuffleboard and hostile driving. Even the county fair was more about rides and the chance to win Jethro Tull coke mirrors than a wholesome celebration of hands-on utility. In high school I fell in love with the Richard Hugo poem "What Thou Lovest Well, Remains American." Hugo was a poet of small-town, working-class America, a burly man with the face of a hard drinker who'd been sucker punched more than once and might have deserved it. He came from the land of real jobs, the kinds of jobs no one around me seemed to have. Reading him by our in-ground pool, I started to form the idea that if a professor's kid who'd never worked anywhere earthier than the mall could be more like Richard Hugo, she might begin to *belong*—to the world of people who did things, who made the country work. Useful people.

By the time I left Florida for graduate school in Ann Arbor, I was primed to fall quickly and deeply into Midwestern Derangement Syndrome. Every bog-standard thing thrilled me: houses made of wood, bulb flowers, more than three kinds of trees! John moved to town six months later and was hit just as hard. For two years we staggered around like tourists, going apple picking and saying "Look, icicles!" to each other. John bought an ancient mint-green Ford pickup with a rusted-out floor. I began wearing enormous hand-knit sweaters over long skirts like my girl crush, Natalie Merchant. Staying on after I graduated was a no-brainer. The only problem was that even Ann Arbor, granola-crunchy as it was, was still a university town where people had inexplicable jobs like "administrator" or "dean." If my hometown was a one out of ten on the Usefulness scale, Ann Arbor was maybe a six. The notion of pushing to, say, an eight gradually took hold, and we contemplated moving out to the country where we could farm, or at least live farmishly. Exactly what that meant wasn't clear, beyond the mental image of large, boisterous dinner parties where guests ate and raved about my home-made bread. That was enough for me, and John was satisfied with the prospect of a barn to paint and sculpt in. We started driving out to the country on weekends to scout locations.

A few months into our farm hunt, an acquaintance of John's mentioned that he had a cottage for rent on his property in Rives Junction, forty-five miles west of Ann Arbor. We visited that weekend and almost collapsed from the thrill of rusticity. Keith, the owner, also lived on the grounds and ran his business out of the renovated barn. He kept llamas, goats, and "show chickens." The hundred-acre property had once been a commercial daffodil and tulip farm, and thousands of flowers still bloomed in columns right behind the cottage, which was bigger than our apartment in town and 30 percent cheaper.

After visiting the farm, we stopped for lunch in Chelsea, the nearest town with a decent restaurant, and agreed that Keith's cottage would be the ideal way to test out country living before taking the plunge into full farm ownership. "It's rustic, but still kind of arty," John said.

"Plus, it has a washer and dryer," I said, raising a forkful of microgreens to my mouth.

We moved to the farm in late spring, that glorious Michigan time between frozen mud and scarring heat, and promptly became euphoric. The daily commute from work in Ann Arbor felt like driving to a vacation home. In the evenings we sat on the back porch and watched bats fly out of the apple trees. My desk looked out onto the flower fields and the woods beyond them. On weekends we visited the llama paddock where Bo, the biggest male, would amble over and let me pet his neck. Bo didn't offer a lot in terms of personality, but he seemed happy enough to hang out with me. A goat named Gretel shared the paddock, and her main shtick was to wiggle out under the split-rail fence, then immediately turn around and stand with her face an inch from the slats, staring fixedly as though wondering how to get back in. I didn't know if that was standard goat behavior, or if Gretel was . . . off. I'm still not quite ready to make the call.

So we were happy in our quarter-life version of *New Zoo Revue*, though there were signs we might not be natural country folk. For instance, we couldn't get cable in Rives Junction, so we spent a considerable amount of time experimenting with where to position our rabbit-eared TV and our bodies to get the best reception. With the TV on the coffee table, John in the very middle of the sofa, and me completing the triangle on the floor, we could sometimes tell Mulder from Scully, Simone from Sipowicz. There was also no pizza delivery where we lived, so one of us had to drive seven miles to the outer edge of the delivery zone and exchange money for pizza in a church parking lot. It was a twenty-mile round-trip to buy the Sunday *New York Times*, thirty miles to see a movie. But it never occurred to us to give any of those things up. So we spent a lot of time in the car.

Rives Junction had also not proved to be as village-like as I'd expected from my extensive reading of British mystery novels. Soon after we moved to the farm, we stopped in at the local pub, ready to banter with the locals or at least watch crabby old men play chess. But the men at the bar sat staring straight ahead, not talking. Dropping off menus, the waitress asked in a friendly enough tone if we were the new people out on Zion Road. We said yes, all smiles.

"Heard you're not married," she said.

"Engaged," I said, reflexively offering my ring hand. But she just smiled tightly and walked away. John and I stared at each other.

"That was weird," I said.

"That was some *Straw Dogs* shit," he replied.

Most of the residents weren't outright rude to our sinful selves, but even the more benign interactions were hard to interpret. One Sunday afternoon at the outset of hunting season, a man in fatigues knocked on the front door to ask if I'd seen anyone take his deer. "I left her right across the road," he said, gesturing to the ditch where I'd picked wild asparagus (or "foraged for food," as I thought of it) in spring. "And when I got back with the truck she was gone." I told him I hadn't seen or heard anything. "Are you sure?" he asked, looking over my shoulder into the living room in a way that made me realize he thought maybe I had taken his deer, dragged her in to bleed out on the sofa.

"Positive," I said apologetically.

His eyes swept the room behind me one more time. "Well, all right," he said with a sigh. "You have a good day, ma'am."

Later, John told me the same man had driven up on an ATV the previous week and tried to give him a kid. "Bet you've been missing this little guy!" the man had said of the toddler. "Found him out back playing with my ducks."

"Hi there," John said to the little boy. "I think you might have the wrong house," he said to the man.

"Are you sure?" the man had said to him.

"Well, yeah."

The man shook his head. "Well, that's the strangest thing. All right. You have a good day now, sir."

I thought maybe it was all part of an elaborate farmhouse-casing scheme, but when I mentioned it to Keith, he shook his head. "Nah, that's just Bill. He lives down the road. He's all right. Just drinks too much." Granted, Keith himself was an odd one. He wore the same clothes every day, frequented tanning parlors, and made cryptic references to things he had seen in Beirut in the 1980s. But I figured he was a better judge of rural weirdness than I was, so if he thought our ATV neighbor was all right, I would, too.

John and I were married that September at an inn an hour west of Rives Junction, christened by the torrential rain that blew in ten minutes before the ceremony and stayed throughout the reception. Winter came soon after, snow making the flower fields as smooth and unbroken as the fondant on our wedding cake. The salt truck came down our road most mornings before dawn, and I drove my little hatchback to work in the slushy ruts it left behind. The drive to town took twice as long in winter. Everything did. Back in Ann Arbor, my method for clearing ice off the car was to get in, turn it on, and sit there listening to PJ Harvey until the windows warmed up enough for the wipers to push everything off. In the country, I was lucky if Keith had been out early and cleared my car along with his own. Other mornings I had to scrape, and hack, and occasionally pour boiling water on the driver-side door to unstick it.

John left for a month at an artists' residency in Vermont. In his letters only a few scant sentences were about his painting; the rest was about the seamlessness of Vermont snow removal. "It's the skiers," he said on the phone. "They can't have ski tourists dying all over the place." Meanwhile, our cottage felt more and more like a snug space pod floating in a sea of whiteness. On my way home from work, I'd stop at the video store fifteen miles outside town, to rent a movie to watch that night, but also to give my hands a break from their iron grip on the steering wheel. For exercise, I bought a mini-trampoline and jogged on it in front of the television. That's how I watched *Schindler's List* for the first time: bouncing.

Spring finally arrived in its usual two-steps-forward-one-step-back way, bringing peonies and mud. I helped Keith's wife, Dorothy, deliver a baby llama, which mostly entailed playing it cool while being utterly certain that mother, baby, and all other animals and humans on the premises were going to die. Then two tawny kittens showed up, all saucer eyes and needle teeth—a gift from Keith to Dorothy, who hadn't been getting along. Before she'd married Keith, Dorothy had been a marketing executive in Detroit, working on auto ads for the Big Three. Now she was bored. She wanted to get back in the game, but Keith said the commute would be too long. I didn't see why that mattered—he wasn't the one who'd be commuting, after all—but it had become a big enough point of contention between them that she was thinking of leaving the marriage altogether. "He's a good man," she'd said. "But a good man isn't enough to make a life on."

The kittens were a peace offering, meant to make life on the farm less lonely for Dorothy. And they were fun to have around, aside from the ringworm they gave us all. But then, less than a month after they arrived, they died. Keith found one in the woods behind the flower fields, dead without a mark on him. I helped Dorothy bury him in a shoe box, holding his brother over my shoulder—ringworm be damned—so he wouldn't see. A week later, the brother went missing, too. John found him in a stand of peonies, his neck broken.

I gave myself some circle-of-life pep talks, but dead

baby animals were just not what I'd bargained for. For the rest of that spring I spent less time at the farm and more in Ann Arbor, which by then, with its one art-house theater and smattering of vegetarian restaurants, felt like the East Village. When I was at home, the farm was so quiet and still that I thought maybe Dorothy had left after all, but she was just spending a lot of time inside.

It was early summer when John called from Ann Arbor to say he'd stumbled on a great house for rent, an A-frame with a sleeping loft and woodstove, two blocks from downtown and pizza and coffee and movies. I protested halfheartedly that we'd barely given rural life a chance, but we both knew I didn't mean it. And winter was coming, at some point. A few weeks later we packed up a U-Haul with Keith's help, unloaded our stuff in the new house, and celebrated with champagne and Caribbean takeout.

"I still can't believe I found this place so fast," John said later that night as we lay in bed.

"What do you mean?" I said. "You weren't looking." Which wasn't entirely true. John's a dedicated real estate window-shopper. He'll go out for a jog anywhere in the world and come back to the hotel with five house flyers. Once in Venice I caught him seriously pondering a listing for a million-euro one-bedroom apartment with marble floors, ancient wiring, and a shared kitchen.

"Of *course* I was looking," he said. "After the kittens were killed I knew it was time to go, even on the remote chance that Keith had anything to do with it."

I just stared at him.

"I thought you knew," he said.

"How would I know that?"

"Because kittens don't just turn up with broken necks."

"I assumed an animal broke their necks," I told him.

"Without leaving any other marks on them?"

"I can't believe you didn't tell me!"

"My priority was getting us out. Besides," he said, "I thought it was tacitly understood."

"It was *not* tacitly understood."

"I see that now."

"Those poor little kittens."

"I know, baby."

John and I stayed in Ann Arbor another ten years, bought a house made of wood, and planted hundreds of bulbs in the yard. Then George W. Bush was reelected. The People's Republic of Ann Arbor was as cozily liberal as ever, but the contrast between those twenty-five square miles and the rest of Michigan got harder to ignore. My drinking, which had become a daily habit soon after 9/11, crept up more as my resentment and frustration grew. Ann Arbor itself began to strike me as increasingly claustrophobic, not to mention a bit smug. "We don't live in the Midwest; we live in *Ann Arbor*," people would say, and I would think about how maybe I didn't want to live in a part of the country where such fine distinctions were necessary. Or maybe it was inevitable that given my tropical childhood, the sight of mud-snow on the ground in April would one day fill me with despair. Maybe I was just done hiding out from the broader lunacy and beauty of the non-cozy world.

The January of Bush's second inauguration, I visited the

West Coast for the first time, barely making it out of heavy snow in Detroit in time to meet John at a conference in San Francisco. The morning after I arrived, we walked to Yerba Buena Gardens and sat in the sun, surrounded by flowering plants from San Francisco's sister cities around the world. On the lawn, elderly Asian women were practicing Tai Chi. Two men walked past us hand in hand.

"Pretty here," John said.

"Yes it is," I said, and burst into tears.

Within a month I had a job interview in Seattle, and within two months we had moved away from the Midwest, away from the snow and tornadoes, away from the leafy bubble that had sheltered us, and to the land of evergreens and grunge and no free parking, ever. I had no idea how I would survive in a big city, where even the parking meters were confusing digital contraptions and my new office building was seventy-six stories tall. But I was willing to table that question for now. I needed mild weather and cultural breathing room and a city full of quirky neighborhoods to explore more than I needed to be Useful. Replanted in Seattle, I imagined myself becoming such a vibrant urban creature that maybe—especially if I could dial down my drinking—I'd find a whole new way to belong.

My second sober summer, my friend Marie sent me a link to a four-day farm camp in eastern Washington with a note: "Want to go?" Which is how I found myself pulling a chicken's heart from its body at 7:00 a.m. in a thunderstorm, wondering if I was still a person with principles or even feelings anymore.

The chickens were that night's dinner, and the idea was for each camper to slaughter her own, thereby feeling more connected to the earth, or the food chain, or at least that one chicken. I had lain awake in bed the night before, agonizing over all the different routes I could choose with my chicken: kill it; don't kill it; don't kill it but still eat it; kill it but don't eat it; kill it but then arrange some kind of blind swap so I wouldn't know if I was eating my chicken or someone else's; kill it and then myself.

Ultimately, I made the worst possible choice, which was to hold and talk to the chicken before it died, let someone else kill it, and rejoin for the evisceration. It was gutless and hypocritical and also in the moment seemed like the only honest path. Because I knew that killing that chicken would not do one goddamn thing to make me feel Useful or close to the earth. I also knew I couldn't admit that to a bunch of near strangers—that I'd feel compelled to fake a solemn awe, when all I'd really be feeling is sorry that I'd ended a life for no real reason. So I spoke softly to the chicken and told myself I was helping it, and after the deed was done, I stuck my hand inside and pulled out its organs.

Then it was 8:00 a.m. and time for breakfast.

I'd known I was in some trouble since the first day, when the campers—all women—gathered for the opening circle. I'm not an opening-circle kind of person. I don't mind the reflecting and the intention setting and the blah-blah-blah; I just don't like packaging it all up in a thirty-second blurb to share with total strangers.

This particular opening circle was like the first chapter of one of those novels where five very different women gather at a spa or class reunion to learn that they aren't so very different after all. The oldest camper said she was going through a divorce and had come to the farm to reconnect with herself. The youngest, a sweet-faced blonde from a family of Napa winegrowers, had just gotten married and felt it was time to "take stock." A freckled thirty-something working to open her own bakery said she came to the farm once a year to remind herself why she does what she does.

We were a group of five, so now only Marie stood between me and my story. I had no idea what I was going to say. I knew that Marie, damn her, was not a huge talker. Fortunately for me, she's also one of the most straightforward people on the planet. She gestured toward one of the camp leaders. "I've taken Kim's cooking classes in Seattle and really enjoyed them, so this seemed like a fun opportunity to get away and learn more from her," she said.

Then it was my turn. If I'd been an opening-circle kind of person, my story would have gone something like this: *I have been sober for fifteen months. I'm awake and responsible and on time. I am a blank slate. I thought I would know who I am by now, what I like, what I can do. I thought I would be more* Useful. *I thought I would have* passions. *Skills. I came here to fall in love with something Useful so I can feel as if I belong on this earth.*

What came out was "I absolutely love goat cheese and thought it would be fun to learn to make it!" Which wasn't a lie, and got me through. And so there we were: the divorcée, the newlywed, the entrepreneur, the hobbyist cook, and the goat-cheese chick, embarking on a voyage of self-discovery.

From a handy-skills perspective, farm camp did not disappoint. We foraged for berries and anise hyssop and pine nuts. (Now that I know what it takes to find and shell a pine nut, I'll never complain about the price again, and neither should you.) We made gnocchi and aioli and wood-fired pizzas. We murdered birds and squeezed goat udders, and I tried persistently but in vain to get the border collies to stop herding goats and pay attention to me. We learned to can, a terrifying process involving glass, tongs, boiling water, and the specter of death—all for a little apricot jam.

And at every turn, my fellow campers seemed to be finding meaning in it. The young newlywed told stories about her family's vineyards and how connected they made her feel to the California seasons. The divorcée said she felt herself opening up. The baker was especially charming in a hyper-Etsy way, describing the yogurt, butter, and even salt she made herself in her studio apartment. I, on the other hand, tried to make meaning. To convince myself I was having an *experience*, the kind of experience only a super-fly, sober, Useful American such as myself could have.

Making fake meaning is exhausting. I mean, at least with canning you end up with something to eat that *might* not kill you. In the afternoon of day three, I snuck away from shelling walnuts and wandered into the orchard. Ayla, a Great Pyrenees whose only apparent farm job was to hang out being awesome, came with me. We sat under a tree for twenty minutes, the longest I'd gone since arriving without the sound of human voices. It was still and very hot, over a hundred degrees. Eventually, things got quiet enough for me to know what I had to do: give up. Give up on this story of me as Useful, or Sober Person Rediscovering the Joy of Life, or *anything* with capital letters. *Can you just be a woman who thought this would be more fun than it is?* I asked myself. *Who wondered how goat cheese is made and, now knowing, is ready to go home?*

In that moment, yes. It turned out I could just exhale all the fakery and return to shelling walnuts as someone with no real feeling for walnuts. So what? They still ended up shelled and ready for pesto, and I breathed with a little less effort.

The ghost of Richard Hugo still nags at me from time to time. At the market I hold a jar of locally made jam—generally some kind of classic/modern mix, like peach spiked with cardamom—and feel a pang of longing for days spent making something so simple and luxurious. The smell of fresh topsoil in spring reawakens my fantasies of a garden with all the plants from the R.E.M. song "Find the River." But I don't run headlong toward grand visions of homespun utility anymore. Instead, I am Useful in small ways: boiling mint and sugar into a syrup for soda, growing thyme and chives on the back porch. I drag my compost bin to the curb. I tell tourists as kindly as possible that I can't direct them to Seattle Grace Hospital because it doesn't exist. There are no amber waves of grain in my life, and I don't think much about whether I belong on this landmass; I just want to belong to the day as it forms around me. Or when I'm feeling ambitious, to the city.

Blackberry

Dear Richard,

An old blue Volvo wagon drove past the window just now and reminded me of the summer I spent in New Hampshire with Ben, your friend, my boyfriend and near-undoing. It was 1990, the summer after sophomore year. Ben and I drank mint juleps and skinny-dipped in frigid creeks and drove his father's hand-me-down Volvo wagon: a car so old that once it started, we were afraid to turn it off, so we kept it running even while buying gas. Ben had spent three consecutive summers reading *Moby Dick*, picking up each year where he'd left off the previous one. I was there that day in June when he stood up naked on a flat rock, shouted *"Finally!* I'm done!" and jumped into the creek, book in hand. You visited us not long after, en route to the Appalachian Trail, and a little part of me wanted to leave with you, because I didn't understand you at all and I was preoccupied (maybe still am) with men I didn't understand.

Back at college that fall you sort of adopted me. Ben had

gone off to grad school in another state, visiting now and then but already drifting toward more convenient women. You and I would cut class and go to the dollar movies, sometimes two in a row. At night you'd show up at my place with a bottle or two of five-dollar red wine. Avia, from Yugoslavia. We'd drink and sometimes you'd unpin the Robert Hass poem "Meditation at Lagunitas" from my corkboard and read it to me. Poetry-reading guys were a dime a dozen at our school, but you were different. You looked like the ex–football player you were—went to the gym twice a day, drove around in a Jeep with roll bars, and never talked about your feelings. And I still didn't understand you or what you wanted from me (though I knew it wasn't sex, which I found mildly insulting). So when you read, I paid attention.

We were earnest English majors. We knew that "Meditation at Lagunitas" was about clinging to the names of things as a way to hold on to what those things represented. For Hass, the word "blackberry" stands in for a whole raft of lost moments. But because we were also twenty-year-old romantics who knew absolutely everything there was to know about longing, pining, and missing, our favorite line was "Longing, we say, because desire is full / of endless distances."

I had spent my whole life longing. In my parents' house, I longed for a place where safety and peace were less tenuous. In our crass, gold-plated Florida town, I longed to live somewhere with changing leaves and old houses and creaky wood floors. I was awkward and embarrassed by every word I said and wanted to feel beautiful and eloquent. I was compulsively cautious and longed for the abandon I imagined from the Prince lyrics that mortified me. I thought back then that the right boy would be my one-stop solution to all of it. Over and over I proved that theory wrong, but I still carried the longing with me, invisible and shifting to fit whoever was around the bend.

At some point I just longed for an end to longing itself. I bought a coffee mug that said, "Bloom Where You're Planted," and every time I filled it, I translated it for myself as *Jesus Christ, can you just be happy for once?* This approach failed, too, and by our year of dollar movies and Robert Hass I was just as susceptible to longing, and also to poetry and wine.

Four years ago I drank my last bottle of wine (not Avia, and not five dollars). For years I had longed to *want* to quit. Then I was just desperate to quit. Once I quit, I longed to drink for what felt like the world's slowest aeon. Then it stopped. *I am a superhero!* I thought. *I can kill longing. From now on I will live in a state of acceptance and joyous contentment.*

I was very impressed with myself. And quite badly mistaken.

This week alone I have longed for the following: lemon ice cream. One more hour of sleep. The smell of rain without the rain itself. A car made of green glass. A private conversation with Emily Dickinson and also one with Grover, the Muppet. My husband's hands on my naked back. Someone else's husband's hands there, too. Blue espadrilles, grilled octopus, the sureness of God, the dog to stop kicking me in his sleep.

So much for joyous contentment.

I got some of these things. But "some" leaves a lot of distance to cross. Last week I reread "Meditation at Lagunitas," and when I got to our favorite line, I thought, *Endless distances. The fucker was being* literal, *and we were too young and dumb to know it.* I texted you: "Robert Hass's endless distances: they're uncrossable, aren't they? I'm never going to cross them and neither are you." You live in Montana now and I pictured you reading my text standing next to a moose.

"Yes," you wrote back. "I mean, no. We're never going to cross them."

"We didn't understand back in 1991," I said. "We didn't understand that longing never stops."

"No," you said. "It's the gun on the mantel in the first act, destined to go off in the third."

I frowned when I read that. How can it be act 3 already, when it feels as if we finished that bottle of Avia ten minutes ago? When I felt like a superhero just five minutes ago? When I want so much more? I have a whole *book* of names standing in for my losses.

"I hope you're assuming a five-act structure," I wanted to respond. But I didn't, because I don't want to know. So please don't tell me.

I was staring at that old Volvo outside the window when I started this letter, and that summer in New Hampshire came flooding back. The buzz of deer flies, the smell of cold water, road trips with Ben in the ancient Volvo wagon that somehow never let us down. Drinking minted bourbon in Adirondack chairs with both of you, in love with Ben but a little with you, too, and thinking I couldn't go wrong either way. Being twenty and so sure that nothing lay ahead but more love and an eventual end to longing.

Now I'm old enough to know better. But I stared out my window at the Volvo and thought, *Maybe if I owned that car, I could feel that way again.* Richard, I'm telling you: I nearly ran out into the street to make an offer, just to close the endless distance.

Notes to Self:
Election Night 2016

The plan is for a quiet celebration. It's not 2008, when your neighborhood pub went insane with joy over Obama's win. When you drank five glasses of Oregon Chardonnay, and the guy on the next bar stool grabbed you and kissed you and John didn't mind because *history* was happening. You expect history to happen tonight, too, and the idea of a woman in the Oval Office is enough to make you swoon, but tonight there will be no boozy group hugs or kisses from strangers. Tonight you'll stay safe, at home, alone in your kitchen because John is out of town. You'll bake cookies to keep yourself busy while the returns come in. It's oddly appropriate: Remember 1992, when Hillary Clinton was all but publicly flogged for saying she didn't stay home baking cookies? Well, now she's about to become president. Who needs booze when you have cookies and vindication?

Revised plan (7:15 p.m. PST):
The plan is to stay calm. Remember that these things

rarely get called early and that the networks have a vested interest in creating suspense. Remember, too, that sobriety means riding out these moments of uncertainty: the mammogram that had to be redone, the job offer you weren't sure you'd get. You've *trained* for times like this. Keep baking and ride it out.

Revised plan (8:00 p.m. PST):

Okay, so the news is getting a little weird. Maybe it's time to stop baking, before distraction makes you confuse salt for sugar or grab a hot tray. The rest of the dough will keep for tomorrow. You can put it in the fridge or just, you know, eat it. Let the dogs lick the beaters. It's important to keep a brave face for the dogs. You know this because the election commentators are no longer keeping a brave face for *you*, and it's freaking you out. Don't let your dogs down the way these people and their stupid pollsters are letting you down. Be glad you're not watching at a bar, where the vibe must be getting sketchy. Be glad that you're here, in your spacious kitchen, in your pretty house, sober, and able to process what is happening rather than spinning out in ten drunk directions.

Revised plan (9:00 p.m. PST):

Just sit on the floor, okay? Just sit down on the fucking floor and try to think. Think small. Don't think about, say, how much America must hate women to let this happen. Don't think about your parents and how happy they must be. Definitely don't google any of the words you want to google right now. Instead, make a list of reasons you will be safe. *White. West Coast. Money. Mobility.* Do everything you can to separate yourself from Them, the people who are in harm's way. You can think this clinically because you're sober, which is different from being brave or kind.

Revised plan (10:00 p.m. PST):

Stay on the floor. It's the best place for you now. Know that the advice your brain is giving you—buy a gun, pull all your money out of the stock market, move into a women's separatist commune—is not helpful. Don't act on any of it right now. Try to stop crying. Know that while you feel crazy right now, may in fact *be* crazy right now, you are sober. If you find yourself saying, *I'm only sober because there's no alcohol in the house,* stop. You've driven through snow-storms, power outages, with fevers or tear-swollen eyes to buy booze, and you could have done it tonight. Nothing stopped you from drinking tonight but you. Because whenever you thought about it—and how could you not?—a voice inside said, *Sure, you could drink. But he will still be president.*

Fascination

John and I were hiking in Ohio's Hocking Hills when I tried to sell him on the upside of AIDS.

"In a weird way, our generation was lucky for getting scared out of casual sex," I began. "We learned to see sex as personal and meaningful. Don't you think?"

"What?" John said. "No. I think we got *cheated*."

"Really? You would rather have slept with tons of people?"

"I would have at least liked the *option*," he said.

I tilted my head. "Why does that surprise me so much?"

"Beats me," John said, and we walked on. Ten years passed before the topic of sexual freedom came up between us again, and by then so much had changed.

In reality, terror of AIDS didn't stop College Kristi from sleeping around. It just subtracted fun and added worry at an age when sex was already more worrisome than fun. In theory, AIDS could have expanded Generation X's formative sexual landscape, given all those PSAs about "other things" we could do that didn't involve penises in vaginas. But the boys in my life had apparently missed those PSAs, because they were deeply, fundamentally obsessed with putting their penises in my vagina. I guess I can't blame them; if I'd had such a direct route to an orgasm, I would have taken it, too.

I went to college not only in the age of AIDS but in the era of "sex-positive feminism," which was a reaction to the idea that pornography and sex work and heterosexual intercourse itself were inherently harmful to women. Being sex positive seemed like a good idea to me. I wanted to be able to fuck guys and shave my legs and wear lipstick without hearing that I was a tool of the patriarchy. And I was all in for taking ownership of my sexual pleasure. Unfortunately, I had no idea how to actually do that. At least not with another person in the room. With other skills, like speaking up in class or dancing in public, a fake-it-till-you-make-it approach had worked well for me. I thought maybe that would work for sex, too, so I set out to rack up some notches on my belt in the diligent, can-do way I'd approached the other stuff. And, because I was newly obsessed with *The Unbearable Lightness of Being*, I took the libertine, garter-belted, no-strings Sabina as my role model.

It was in this way that I had a bunch of sexual experiences that were variously friendly and sweet and weird and creepy and fun but never actually hot. I was so busy performing the role of a cool, sex-positive chick that I forgot it was supposed to be about what got *me* off, too. I suppose I thought if I just kept at it, the things boys liked would become the things I liked. In the meantime, I had sex as an out-of-body experience (and not in a good way) and told myself that just meant I was focused on the right stuff: the heart, the soul.

I tried hard to be a Sabina but inevitably backslid into my true nature as her gentler, more traditional counterpart, Tereza. That's how I ended up with a boyfriend—and not just any boyfriend but one who had also read Kundera and was (unfortunately) striving to live as Tomas, the distant, womanizing protagonist. We met midway through my freshman year in college. "It's you," Ben said when a friend introduced us. "I've been looking for you." A sultry poem of mine had been published in the college literary quarterly, and he'd set his sights on its author. I could feel him sizing me up from where he lay sprawled on our friend's couch. He had a sharp nose and light eyes that didn't seem to blink a lot, or give much away. I couldn't tell from the way he looked at me if he liked what he saw. Even when he was inside me three days later, I wasn't sure.

The friend who'd introduced us sighed when I told her I'd slept with him. "I don't know if Ben likes women or just women's bodies," she said.

"He said he finds me *fascinating*," I told her. "Absolutely fascinating" were the exact words he'd used as we lay in his bed afterward, but I didn't want to brag.

She just shook her head and smiled. "Well, I hope at least the sex is good."

It wasn't, at least not for me. Ben was a self-styled so-phisticate, always giving me Marguerite Duras books to read and red wine to drink. But in bed, the twenty-year-

old boy held sway. Whether he liked me was still some-
what mysterious, but he definitely liked my body, or at
least pieces of it. He would play with my nipples long
enough to drive me half out of my mind with rapture and
then leave me at that halfway point as he thudded away
inside me, came silently, and rolled off. We seemed to have
a tacit understanding that my pleasure came from en-
abling his—that I came through his orgasms, like a sexual
stage mom.

I say it *seemed* like a tacit understanding because as a sex-
positive young miss, I did not agree. I knew my orgasms
mattered, too. I'd been having them on my own since
middle school and had even managed them on occasion in
the company of men. But the men who had made me come
(simply by caring enough to give it a real shot, not out of
some special wizardry) tended to be kind of . . . not what I
considered boyfriend material. One of them had run away
from home and was living in an abandoned moving van;
one was rumored to be AWOL from the army; one liked
to do it in parked cars in broad daylight. Now that I had a
boyfriend, I knew I deserved to be having orgasms, and I
knew it was partly up to me to make it happen.

What I needed was for Ben to go down on me. But even
though I spent a lot of time with his cock in my mouth, he
had never shown the slightest indication that he knew cun-
nilingus was a thing. For a while I assumed it was bound
to happen eventually. Maybe he just needed to get to know
me better. But a year into our relationship, his mouth had
barely gotten to belly-button level. I was vaguely paranoid
that my nether regions might be somehow gross, but I was

also self-aware enough to know that was a run-of-the-mill girl worry, not reality. (And anyway, it's not as if semen were such a delight to taste, either.) *Maybe I just need to somehow be sexier*, I thought. But how? I was already on a constant diet to try to be more like the waifish girls he openly preferred. I was already up for fucking him anytime, anywhere. I couldn't understand how my sheer willingness wasn't doing the trick.

And I also really, really didn't want to talk about it. Not with him. But I did mention it to my friend Nina one day. She was seeing a new guy, and they'd had "an oral sex *fiesta*" earlier that week. "After the third time I practically had to kick him in the head to get him off me," she said.

"Ben doesn't do that," I told her.

"Do you want him to?" she asked. Well, yeah. "Then you'd better find out what his problem is."

The next time Ben seemed nice and relaxed after a blow job, I brought it up. "I guess I'm just curious about why. It's not a big deal or anything," I lied. "It's just something I've enjoyed when other guys have done it."

I used the "other guys" line because Ben did take an interest in what I'd done in the past. For instance, a few months into our relationship he was fucking me on my dorm room floor and suddenly pinned both my wrists above my head. "Do you like it when other guys do this?" he asked.

"I don't know," I said, because no one had ever done it before. I could tell from the little throb it gave me that I didn't dislike it, and maybe I should have just said *yes, yes, I like it.* Maybe I missed my chance to bust things wide open. But I wasn't so great at thinking on my feet (or my back) in those days. He took my "I don't know" as a no, or just a lack of interest, and never tried it again.

This time I really did have data from other guys to fall back on, but it didn't help. Ben thought for a minute and then said, "I just don't like doing it."

"So you've tried it before?" I said.

"Yeah. I just don't like it."

This was more or less what I said whenever Ben presented me with the perfect oyster that he swore would make me love the slimy, salty things. *I just don't like them.* But he kept trying. Maybe I should have kept trying, too, or at least probed further. *But you haven't tried with me*, I could have said. Or, *You could learn to like it.*

Instead, I said, "Oh. Okay." And that was the end of it.

Well, almost. A year later, we were still together but living five hundred miles apart. The first night he visited me from grad school, Ben pulled my jeans down and then licked me twice, sort of near my clit. He came back up beaming. "I love you so much," he said. And my body and brain shut right down. First, because I already knew he was a chronic cheater, and this was proof that some other woman had talked him into what I could not. Second, because he never used modifiers like "so much," which made me suspect he'd been cheating even more than normal. And third, because I didn't want him to lick me as an act of loving self-sacrifice. I wanted him to lick me because he wanted to watch me implode.

But my expectations of both Ben and myself were pretty low by that point, and I didn't want to ruin the visit with a fight. So I acted pleased, and our relationship staggered on another six months. A few weeks after we finally split up, I got up the nerve to make a play for John, who'd been on my radar at our small college for years. We'd met my first night on campus but had never been more than friendly acquaintances. I'd kept tabs on him, though: on his artwork and his much-mythologized wild streak and his gorgeous girlfriend, who did things like smash plates on the floor if she thought he was looking at another woman. John had graduated a year ahead of me and now lived in his painting studio in a sketchy neighborhood. He drank a lot and generally smelled like turpentine. He wasn't boyfriend material. But he was the right level of scary to make him a fun rebound man. I chatted him up at a party one night and then drove him home. We made out in his painting studio, and then he was kneeling on the floor between my legs. "Kristi," he said quietly. "If I give you head, will you come?"

"I don't know," I said, because I didn't, and because I was already too wobbly with desire to lie.

"Well, can I try?"

Five years later we were married. And not only because he made me come often and hard. Also because John had turned out to be *spectacular* boyfriend material. Yes, he drank. Yes, he had a temper that left at least one hole in our walls before he went to therapy and got a handle on it. But he treated me like a superhero princess and was also warm, responsible, hilarious, and kind to children and animals. All his exes still talked to him. He loved his mother but saw the real person inside her. His worst habit (besides the drinking, which was a plus at the time) was falling in love with and buying decrepit old trucks.

When we married, I breezed right through the "forsaking all others" vow because of *course* I was forsaking all others. Why would I—why would any woman—ever need anyone but John in her bed/shower/kitchen/yard? We exchanged rings, and I settled in for a lifetime of happy, orgasmic monogamy.

And that's what I got: the kind of marriage I'd never seen growing up and had barely realized was available to me. The kind with sex and laughter and travel and generally enough money and gifts for no reason and also breathing space. Sure, I was attracted to other men and vice versa from time to time, but that was barely a blip on the radar. *You've still got it*, I'd think when I felt a man's attention on me. But I wasn't going to use it on anyone but John. Drinking gets a lot of people into extramarital trouble, but not me. The more I drank, the more I clung to him: my safe space, my non-judgment zone, my, what's the word— enabler.

It was all so simple. And then, seventeen years into marriage, I stopped drinking.

It went something like this:

1. I got sober.
2. Getting sober made me like myself.
3. Liking myself made me feel powerful.
4. Feeling powerful made me feel sexy.
5. Really sexy.
6. And I wanted to share it with the world.

I didn't actually run around seducing all and sundry; most of the action took place in my head. But there was still a lot of it. For instance, I started to evaluate the men I interacted with on a daily basis as potential sex partners. Not in a hot-or-not sense. I didn't sort them into Yes and No columns. I just . . . wondered. In meetings or bookstores or restaurants: *What would he be like? Or him? What's he into?* (This is also when I realized just how far on the heterosexual side of the spectrum I fall, because my thoughts almost never landed on women, and at the time I was open to *everyone*.) I also developed a mild fixation on penises. I'd be chatting with someone about his vacation plans or a work project while simultaneously wondering what his dick looked like.

I didn't know exactly what was going on, but I had a couple of theories. Knowing that people in recovery commonly transfer their old addiction to a new one (cigarettes for alcohol, candy for cigarettes, marathons for candy), I thought maybe my mental sluttiness was just a new source of dopamine, an upgraded addiction. But mostly, I think I was just learning how to want. I'd spent so much youthful energy turning myself into a sexual blank slate who could transform under any man's gaze. Sober, I started gazing back, and I saw that my desire for a man could match or even topple his for me. I saw that men weren't the only ones who wanted to possess what they knew deep down they could never own. That I, too, longed to kiss and bite and fuck myself as close to it as possible.

I tried to pour most of what I termed my Newfound Rapacity back into my marriage. My happy marriage.

Somehow we'd grown from broke, hard-drinking young bohemians into settled, teetotaling forty-somethings without losing the seeds of ourselves or our coupledom. Sure, we drifted apart from time to time in the way that any two people with big jobs and individual passions will do, but we always drifted back together. "Marriage is wide," we said, meaning it should be able to accommodate our separateness—his surf trips on the coast, my solo nights at rock shows, each of our consuming careers the other couldn't fully understand—as well as our two-ness. Sex had always been a big thing for us, and sobriety had amped things up in both quality and variety. My Newfound Rapacity bumped it up one more notch. But I held something back. I didn't want John to know about the 24-7 gleam in my eye; he might wonder where it had come from, and I didn't know how to explain. And I really didn't want him to know that I was tempted to get out there and enjoy some of the casual sex we'd been, in his words, cheated out of as young adults. So I (mostly) behaved myself without trying to suppress what I'd uncovered. And I kept it a secret from John. Secrets were nothing new to me; I'd been keeping them since childhood, in part to protect myself from parents who thought my feelings belonged to them. When I was a teenager, my mother read my diary and used the details against me, so I started keeping a shadow diary in my head. Now I started a new shadow diary for my sexual self in hope that eventually my feelings for other men would seem so natural that I could overlook them, or at least redirect them toward my husband.

My plan worked *great*. I gazed, and fantasized, and

(mostly) stayed on the right side of the line I was toeing. Until I met someone I didn't even contemplate fucking, because I couldn't get past the more immediate urge to kiss him for a hundred hours.

His name was Noah and he was just a guy from work. Smart and cute and fun, qualities I registered without the ding-ding-ding that means I'm in trouble—maybe because he was married, maybe because he was in his early thirties and I tended to gravitate to older men. Noah and I worked on a project together and hit it off in that work-friend way. We had hallway chats about movies and running, which gradually turned into hallway chats about how movies and running made us feel, which turned into longer conversations about how travel and solitude and meditation made us feel. At a company mixer we leaned against the wall for an hour talking about people close to us who had died. Co-workers would drift by, beers in hand. *Hi!* we'd say. *We're talking about death.* The co-worker would move on, and we'd get right back to it. Our shared project had ended, and now it seemed we had picked up a new project of learning each other.

One day in late fall we hugged in the lobby of our building, and my body lit up. Not just the sex parts, or even primarily the sex parts. The whole thing: elbows, hair. A whole circuit of light. It was far from our first hug, and after we parted I stared at the floor wondering why this one had been different. I still don't know. But I decided it was fine. After all, I gazed *back* now. I was *allowed* to notice the ding-ding-ding when it occurred.

Noah and I had started going out for coffee now and

then, which turned into every other week, and then every week. We always met at the same café and sat in side-by-side armchairs in the front window. We made small talk about work for thirty seconds, and then one of us would say, "So do you believe in God?" Or, "Do you feel like there's enough art in your life?" And we'd just get lost—in each other, in the world of ideas, in whatever we weren't talking about with our spouses, because who doesn't already know if his or her own spouse believes in God? The armchairs were low-slung, and as our conversation deepened, we'd slump down in them so that to make eye contact, we had to turn our heads to the side, like two people lying in bed.

I had a dream that we got locked in the café overnight, and he made me a grilled cheese sandwich, and then we had sex for hours before falling asleep in the armchairs. "I dreamed we got locked in the café!" I texted him. "You made me a sandwich and then we fell asleep in the red chairs." I couldn't mention the sex, but by then I suspected he would know.

Ordinary moments between us took on an unacknowledged intensity. In the café, I sometimes caught myself staring at his hands around his coffee cup. Or he'd say something banal like "I'm going to grab a lid, you want one?" "No thanks," I'd say and then we would stare helplessly at each other for an awkwardly erotic number of seconds. It was mortifying. It was wonderful. So were our hugs—especially the goodbye hugs, which were long and close enough for me to notice that if I wore three-inch heels, our torsos lined up perfectly. A better woman would have stopped wearing three-inch heels to coffee, but I had no interest in being a better woman.

Well, almost none. I knew that all the time I spent with or thinking about Noah was supposed to be a symptom of problems in my marriage, so I spent a lot of my downtime trying to diagnose them. But I couldn't come up with much. I was having a wonderful life with John, and John seemed to be having a wonderful life with me. True, I never asked John if he had enough art in his life, or how he felt about his parents' marriage, but only because I already knew. I didn't know these things about Noah, and it seemed important to find out, and I didn't see why I shouldn't have this little excavation project on the side.

"I know this is supposed to mean I need to work on my marriage, but I think I just need to work on *myself*," I told my friend Claire.

"When married women have feelings for someone else, they're always told it means they need to do more *work*," Claire said. "Maybe nothing's wrong. Maybe you're just having a human experience."

"I'm about to ask an awkward question," I told Noah a few weeks later. It was late April, and for once the sun was out. We'd taken our coffees to a small park where two homeless men bickered about cigarette money a few feet away. "Do you think we might be having, like, a *human experience* with each other?" I'd asked because I had to. The stares were getting longer, the hugs closer. Without conscious thought, I'd found my hand in his hair during the last one, and he didn't act as if there were anything strange about that. Plus, we'd begun to complain (mildly, but still) about our spouses and to opine about how marriage—not *our* marriages, you understand, but the Institution—was too limiting to contain a person's whole self. It was time for someone to pull the Band-Aid off.

I thought he would know what I meant by "human experience," and I was right. "Yes," he said, and we both exhaled audibly.

"I thought it might just be me," I said, partly to say something and partly because I really had thought there was a 10 percent chance that this was some delusional-old-lady *Death in Venice* deal.

"No," Noah said, and we lapsed into a comfortable silence. We kept staring at each other, but even the staring felt softer now that it had an acknowledged cause. After a minute or two we began trading fragmented thoughts back and forth:

I don't want to fuck up your life.

That one day. I sat there and thought, What is happening to us?

I don't want to fuck up your life, either.

Any bit of myself I give to you, I'd be taking from my marriage.

It could never end well. Even if it started well.

Are hearts that zero-sum? Never mind. It doesn't matter.

And it would definitely start well.

She already suspects something's up.

If we were single, this would make so much sense.

He has no idea I'm even capable of this.

I think I have to be careful around you.

That's what hurts. That it makes so much sense.

And yet you fascinate me. I'm fascinated by you.

From the outside it probably sounded as coherent as the chatter from the homeless guys. From the inside, only a little more. Finally, we fell silent again, and then he leaned in toward me and said, "Do you think you could stay in control of this? Because I don't. I have no illusions that I could have an affair with you and keep it under any kind of control."

Oh, God, I wanted to say yes. I thought of all the men I could say yes to and mean it. I knew I had it in me, the ability to take a lovely, funny, good man and keep him in a compartment for alternate Wednesdays only. Shamelessly, even joyfully. A few of the men I could say yes to flashed in my mind as I looked at him.

"No," I said. "I couldn't control it. I would fall in love with you."

When we parted, we hugged as if our lives depended on it, as usual, and then backed off until it was something different: two people standing very still with their arms around each other. I could feel his belly against mine. I rested my forehead on his chest.

"I don't want to be this kind of person," I said.

"You're not any kind of person," he said. "You're just Kristi."

For a month we met for long conversations about why we obviously could not have an affair, interspersed with long looks and occasional tears. There was the chance of greater hurt. There was the decade-plus age difference, though I was the only one who cared about that. There was the fact that we worked together. There was the knowledge that pain was bound to follow. And then there were our marriages. His was in a rough patch, but he could see a path back to happiness. Mine *was* happy, which hadn't stopped me from marching into this thing. But neither one of us was looking for an exit.

There were all these great reasons to walk away. And then there was the love. That's how we talked about it, as a thing. We didn't say we loved each other. We'd bought houses and had lives with other people; we weren't dumb enough to think a few months of sneaking around like teenagers could be talked about in the same way. But love was in the room like an end table or umbrella stand, and we let it be. "I have strong feelings of love when I sit here with you" was how he put it once. He had them. We had them.

The day Noah told me definitively that he needed to focus on his marriage, I decided I hated want and desire and love. They were as painful as a side stitch, and no more special or noble. "I want to give everything back," I told him. "I don't want this potential to feel stuff anymore."

"Yes you do," Noah said.

"No," I said. "I've had enough new love for one life. I'm deciding that now. No more."

He leaned into me and smiled. "But that's not the kind of life we're going for, remember?"

He was one of the most authentically optimistic people I'd ever known; just the way he said the word "future" could float a gold haze over me. "I'm so optimistic I get blind-sided by the obvious," he'd said early in our friendship. I remembered that now. I wondered what would blindside him next, now that it wasn't going to be me.

Afterward I walked to the Olympic Sculpture Park and sat by the water. I'd long assumed that if I wandered outside our marriage, I'd keep it to myself unless there was some greater good from telling John. But that was in a hypothetical zipless-fuck scenario, where I had my fun and danced away. I knew that kind of dalliance was still a possibility for me, but I also realized now that it might not be as zipless as I'd assumed, because as much as I wanted to be purely rapacious, my heart might insist on butting in. I had fallen in love with Noah, and I might fall in love again someday; in fact, I probably *would*, unless I arranged my life so that falling in love was impossible.

And Noah was right. A life where falling in love was impossible was not what I was going for, not after the effort of dragging myself from addiction back to the land of the living and feeling.

That weekend I sat in our living room watching John read the paper. "Can I tell you something that scares me?" I blurted.

"Of course," John said, and waited to hear one of my usual fears: cancer or earthquakes or the total illegalization of women by the U.S. government.

"I'm feeling sad that the part of my life that included falling in love is just *over*," I said, with a sense of diving into rapids.

He smiled. I hadn't expected that. "What makes you think it is?"

"I mean the part where I could fall in love even a little bit without it being a catastrophe. Because of, you know, this." I waved my hands around to indicate "marriage."

John put his paper down. "Well, 'catastrophe' is a strong word," he said. "Things aren't that black-and-white."

He wasn't getting it. Time to be more direct. "The thing is, someone has feelings for me." He nodded and waited. "And I like it. I really, really like it." I'd intended to give him the broader context, to tell him about the part where I gazed back, where I did more than just enjoy being desired, but I started to cry before I could get there.

Later, I'd tell him a lot more. About the flirting and trying to have X-ray penis vision. About how it felt to finally know how to *want*. About my feelings for Noah. I told him all (okay, many) of the secret thoughts I'd been keeping so he would never have to know his wife thought about anyone else. Or, rather, so *I'd* never have to face him knowing it. So I could stay in the box he'd never asked me to live in. And in and around this conversation we laughed a lot and cried a little and had tons of sex, and I emerged both dizzy with new freedom and more in love with him than ever. And more ready for a future where I would have to make decisions and be accountable for them, with no booze or hangovers to take the blame.

But in that moment, all I had was "I really, really like it" and trembling hands.

John came to sit by me on the sofa, and I made myself look him in the eye.

"Do you hate me?" I asked.

He smiled, his eyes made a slightly paler blue with tears in them. "You're asking if I hate you for being a woman with a fuckload of unruly feelings?"

I nodded.

"*No*, I don't hate you," he said. "Jesus, baby. Why would I want anything else?" And I stared at him, enthralled.

Elephant Gray

It was my fiftieth day without a drink, and I thought I deserved a congratulatory treat. A cupcake, maybe. I bought one with Neapolitan icing and a cherry on top and ate it while tentatively marveling at my own awesomeness. Then, heading back to the car, I passed Barneys. I didn't need anything from Barneys, but I figured I should go in anyway and just, you know, make sure everything was all right. I started my inspection just inside the front door, in Handbags. My eye fell on a pebbled-leather Belstaff bag in an unusual brownish-gray color. I picked it up, put it back, picked it up again, and stood in front of a mirror checking it out against my body. A salesman walked over. "Isn't it gorgeous?" he said. "A perfect elephant gray."

I looked in the mirror again, turned to the side and back. The bag was heavy, beautifully made, and like no other I owned. It was also seventeen hundred dollars. But it was my fiftieth day without a drink, and I deserved a congratulatory treat. I smiled at the salesman. "I'll take it," I said.

This could be a story about how I recovered from alcoholism by transferring my addiction to spending, ruining my financial life in the process. But it isn't, because I had the money to spend on a seventeen-hundred-dollar bag. I got sober as what most people would call "rich," a word that I can't quite own. But "wealthy," or "affluent," or just "privileged"? Yes. I drank that way, too, and it's true: money changes everything.

I grew up middle-class, a professor's kid. We always had decent cars and new shoes and trips to Disney World. I always knew I would go to college and assumed I would get some kind of job and earn a decent living. But I was never supposed to make *this* much money. I don't mean that in an existential, I-don't-deserve-it way. I mean that my employer literally never intended to pay me this much money. The company's compensation model involves a smallish salary rounded out with stock shares that together are supposed to add up to a competitive package. And that was true for the first few years, before the value of those shares started to go, as the finance world would put it, batshit. The shares I own today are twenty-two times as valuable as the ones I was given when I was hired, making me significantly overpaid for what would still be a high-earning job elsewhere. "You do realize that no other company will pay you this much money," my financial adviser reminds me, eyebrows raised, every time I make noises about quitting over the stress or because I'm sick of tech bros or because I just want a change. And though I roll my eyes when he says it, telling him *of course* I know that, in truth it's always a surprise. After a decade like this, I've forgotten it isn't normal. I feel as if I deserve every penny.

In some ways my drinking escalated in parallel to my affluence, because my affluence escalated in parallel to my misery at work. Before Seattle, I worked at a sleepy company in Ann Arbor that paid me decently and promoted me every couple of years. Seven years in, I was bored. So when I was recruited by my current employer, I was ripe for the picking. I asked some blunt questions first, of course, because even in 2006 the company culture was associated with unpleasant phrases like "meat grinder." "I'm not looking to get *divorced*," I told my future boss during the interview, and he quickly assured me that the company's reputation as a destroyer of lives and marriages was exaggerated. In years to come, I saw co-workers vote not to hire a candidate who even mentioned the concept of work-life balance, so I guess I got lucky.

For a couple of years I existed in a state of controlled panic as I tried to master my new job. I was surrounded by smart, warm, kind colleagues in varying states of collapse. One woman frequently broke out in hives. Another was losing her hair. My office mate came back to our tiny, windowless space from meetings with the senior vice president shaking with nerves and fury, telling me how the SVP had demanded to know where another team member had gotten his M.B.A. and then said, "Stanford? I don't believe it. You're too stupid." We all felt stupid, whether anyone was calling us that or not. We were lifelong overachievers who'd landed in a place where it was nearly impossible to overachieve, dredging up whatever childhood issues had made us so desperate to impress in the first place. If you looked closely, you could see our preteen selves trembling beneath our skin. I was already a daily drinker when I moved to Seattle, but my two glasses of wine became three within months of starting my job.

But it was a genuinely exciting place to work. We were there to solve big problems, the CEO told us, and it was true. At my old company my job stayed largely the same year to year, and when I asked for more, I was mildly chided for being too ambitious. Now I was swimming in more opportunities than even a few thousand overachievers could tackle at once. And we were expected to tackle all of them.

And then there was the money. For the first couple of years, it wasn't such a big deal. I'd gotten a comfortable bump in salary when I left Michigan, but Seattle was also much more expensive than Ann Arbor. And Michigan was apparently the canary in the housing-bust coal mine, so John and I were stuck paying rent *and* a mortgage for the year it took our house to sell at a loss. But when the stock vests started to kick in, the stress and pain and generally grim work conditions paid for Italian vacations and shoe sprees and all the new hardcover books my heart desired, with money left over for retirement, or what some people called a "walking away" fund. I called it the "fuck you" fund, which says something about the kind of angry rich person I was starting to become.

Because as my net worth grew, my worldview shrank. I'd worked my way into bigger responsibilities and more exposure to senior leadership, where I, too, had the envied opportunity to have VPs fling the word "stupid" at me. My next big milestone would be promotion to the executive ranks. But the company's promotion process was largely secret, and no one could really tell me what I needed to *do* to be worthy. One boss said my job performance was already there, but my role wasn't big enough. The next said my role was big enough, but I needed to be better at it. As years passed and I didn't get the tap on the shoulder, I became obsessed with what I saw as my own overwhelming failure to achieve. Every decision I made hinged on whether it could get me promoted. Every time I walked into a room of executives, I imagined them thinking what a disappointment I had turned out to be. Finally, when I'd landed in the biggest role of my career and nailed it, I used the temporary halo to cue up one more discussion with my VP about what I needed to do to make the leap. He smiled benevolently. "Just change the world," he said, opening his hands wide, "and it will be an easy sell."

Just change the world. My three glasses of wine a night became four.

And I stayed. Because I wanted excitement and the hunt for approval more than I wanted peace or comfort or self-confidence. I stayed because I was convinced by that point that no other company would want me. And I stayed because of money. Because I liked the things it bought. Because the things it bought helped me lie to myself about my drinking and, you know, my *soul*. Nearly everyone I worked with drank a lot, and we drank well—rare scotches, fancy liqueurs, excellent northwestern wines that helped us pass off boozing as being locavores. I joined a local wine club that delivered four curated bottles directly to my desk every month. On business trips, I sought out fancy hotel bars as peaceful places to catch up on e-mail while steadily getting lit. As my drinking and my unhappiness escalated, I threw money at anything that would ease the burdens of daily living. Housecleaning, gardening, grocery delivery, first-class flights: I became an expert at spotting and removing any source of friction in my life. And once I'd begun drinking enough to scare myself, I started to spend money on anything that I thought might help me dial it back without requiring me to actually quit: yoga retreats, hypnotherapy, Reiki, craniosacral work, psychic readings. All of these things were enjoyable, and had their small benefits, but they didn't fix me as I wanted them to, and the practical middle-class girl inside me was embarrassed to be spending thousands of dollars on solutions that were ephemeral at best. But it also made sense, because the problem I was trying to solve was my soul, which I believed had broken down for mysterious reasons that had nothing to do with my drinking. If I could only buy the right goods or services to put my soul back together, then I might reach a state of serenity where work and life would feel manageable. And *then*, as a side benefit, I would also get my drinking back under control.

That was the plan, anyway. What actually happened was a more dramatic version of the plan in reverse. When it became clear that no amount of money thrown at unconventional healers was going to stop me from continuing to break into shards, I quit drinking. In the weeks and months after I quit, I continued to fling money around (I didn't stop being me, after all). But I spent it on smaller indulgences: a stack of fashion magazines to read in the backyard during the hours I used to spend drinking, or a film festival pass to put some structure around my dangerously open weekends. I bought myself flowers and mystery novels and other gifts suitable for someone recuperating from a long illness. Choosing these things, I sometimes felt as though I were shopping for a stranger I had a crush on. *Which flowers?* I'd ask myself at the farmers' market. *Do you want the peach ones? How about the coral? What do you like? Who are you?*

Without wine to erase each day, it also became apparent within a few months that the Dalai Lama himself wouldn't be able to tolerate the clusterfuck of conflicting goals, wildly careening priorities, and unrealistic expectations that constituted my work life. *It's not me*, I thought one day. Or not *just* me, at any rate. There was bona fide madness all around me and I wanted out.

When I realized that my job was toxic to me, and that I wanted to stay sober, and wanted to be able to breathe and think and survey the new life I'd uncovered, I changed teams, moving to a role that gave me the space I needed. Still, I was sometimes haunted by the absence of panic in my life. If I wasn't choking on work, I felt as if I weren't doing my job, as though fear and paranoia were part of the description. One day I had coffee with a VP I'd known for years and confessed this to her. "I like my job," I said, leaning across the table and lowering my voice just in case the Starbucks was bugged. "But it's kind of *easy* and I feel bad about that."

She raised an eyebrow and spoke in full voice, hidden mikes be damned. "*Never* feel guilty for taking an easy job now and then. It's the only way to sustain a career in this place. You have to have times where you just coast."

I still work for the company that proved such a friendly breeding place for my addiction. I've been around long enough to know which parts of it are hospitable to health and sanity and which are not. Even in the sane places, I see the usual types: the star performer who lives in terror of being fired; the perfectionist who promises his worried manager that he's only working fifty hours a week when he's secretly putting in seventy; the one who won't stay home when she's sick, setting off round-robins of illness across the team; the one who catches up on e-mail at 1:00 a.m. At some point the company realized it's too hard to recruit and keep employees when you treat them like contestants on a Darwinian game show, and in the last couple of years measures have been put in place to make things better. But policies change faster than cultures. The most wild-eyed ones around me don't yet know it's safe to catch their breath. Or they're chasing a fascinating idea or on a mission to make something crazy sounding that in ten years the world will think it can't live without. Or they just can't walk away from all that fucking money.

As the Barneys salesman rang up my fiftieth-day treat, I started to feel ashamed of myself for buying something so expensive on impulse, and for such an arbitrary milestone. I looked at the clerk, a handsome man with salt-and-pepper hair. He was cheerful and friendly, but maybe he secretly hated me, I thought. Maybe he was inwardly shaking his head over the kind of crazy woman who gets giddy over a bag the color of an elephant. I wondered how much money Barneys paid him, and if he liked working there, and if it was what he'd expected to be doing with his life. Finally, to halt the shame spiral and break the silence, I said, "This is to celebrate my fiftieth day without a drink."

He looked up from wrapping my bag, beamed, and stuck out his hand. "That's *wonderful*," he said. "Congratulations. I have six years." And we shook hands. I thought of him every time I carried the Belstaff bag. Eventually, I got tired of elephant gray. But I keep it around to remind me.

Happy Sometimes

I woke that day in Paris with a wine headache and the sense I'd lost something forever. My dog Abby, who had died three weeks earlier, had visited me in my sleep. There were smells; there were licks. There was sun on my head. She bounded off happily at the end and didn't look back. It was comforting to sense that wherever she was, she didn't need me anymore. But I also knew she was gone for good now.

I sat up in bed and cried for a few minutes, and then I went and stood by the floor-to-ceiling window. My room was on the eighteenth floor of the hotel, with views of the Eiffel Tower and the Arc de Triomphe. It was a mild Saturday in June with peonies blooming everywhere. I had the whole weekend free for exploring.

God, I hate this city, I thought.

I didn't find Parisians ruder than people in any other large, tourist-swamped city. They were fine—meaner than Romans, nicer than New Yorkers. I didn't think Paris was particularly dirty or covered in dog poop, either. In fact, it was the most mathematically, precisely beautiful place I'd ever seen. But that kind of splendor seemed to have no room for an asymmetrical someone like me.

Even Parisian love left me in the margins. As I walked or jogged through the Tuileries, couples kissed passionately on either side of the path. I had been married for twelve years, happily, but the odds of ever being kissed like that in public again were slim; it just doesn't happen to wives (or so I thought then). Intellectually, I knew that I'd had my day, had done my share of making out on park benches with someone who simply *could not wait* for a more dignified opportunity, but I could not for the life of me remember what it felt like. And that was enough to make me resent the whole city for reminding me my days of irresistibility were over.

It didn't help that my three trips to Paris had all been for work, and my company's French headquarters was one of the least inspiring places on earth. The physical setting was aggressively unlovely, like a 1970s IBM office. The team I was working with had been so low on the totem pole for so long that it was baked into their very cells. Every day there was an endless stream of last-minute assignments and issues to untangle. In Tokyo, Seattle, or Munich, my constituency would embody the same polite sadness and resignation, only in Paris it was less polite, more baleful. They barely looked at me when I talked.

I stared out the hotel window, feeling sorry for myself for having to be in one of the world's most romantic cities without any chance of feeling swoony or swooned over again, for having a non-immortal dog and a thankless job and a headache that I could only blame on myself. It was clear that if I didn't get dressed and leave the hotel, I would end up lying on the bed all afternoon, watching CNN International and weeping.

There must be one *thing you'd like to go see today*, I told myself. On previous trips I'd visited Sainte-Chapelle and the Musée d'Orsay, in keeping with my preference for second-tier tourist sites with short lines. The only place I really wanted to go was home. *Okay*, I said to myself the way I'd spoken to Abby after I knew she was very sick but before I realized she might die. *Then what would make Paris feel most like Seattle?*

An hour later I was in the Village Voice bookshop in Saint-Germain-des-Prés. Like any decent bookworm, I'd been to the more famous Shakespeare and Company before but found it too crowded with other people like me to be very browsable. The Village Voice wasn't a tourist destination, just a store crammed with books in English. My eyes filled with tears when I walked in, though to be fair, my eyes had also filled with tears twice on the Metro ride over and once on my walk down Rue Princesse, just because.

I spent a few minutes at the new-book table, striving to establish myself as a normal woman rather than the kind who wandered around Paris crying. Then, suitably impressed with what I'd seen, I went to the fiction shelves and found the *C*s for the litmus test I give every new bookstore: Does it stock Laurie Colwin novels? I firmly believe that without at least one Colwin novel or story collection on its shelves, a bookstore can be good but not great. Most bookstores fail the Colwin Test. The Village Voice had *all* of her books. I pulled my favorite, *Happy All the Time*, off the shelf and opened to the first page: "Guido Morris and Vincent Cardworthy were third cousins." Just seeing the words made my heart skip a beat and lose a little of its weight. I bought eight books at the Village Voice, and that was one of them.

Laurie Colwin published four novels, three story collections, and two books of cooking essays before her sudden death from a heart attack at age forty-eight. Many people know her best for her food writing—and it's great—but I love her as the creator of a warm, sparkling fictional world where everyone is smart and funny, New York feels as cozy as a college town, and love causes just the right amount of pain. Colwin wrote mostly about young WASPs from old-money families. In classic old-money style her characters tend to be inconspicuous consumers; they dress shabbily and eat simple, bland food. But the signs of a vast safety net are all around them. They work industriously, but their jobs are at obscure academic journals or boutique publishers or other places where it is hard to earn an actual urban living. They live in small Village walk-ups, but their galley kitchens contain only gleaming copper cookware. I suspect most of them were taught how to sail as children. In Colwin's world, wedding lunches and art openings happen, with tipsy misbehavior and family arguments and seasons of ennui, but rarely death or divorce and *never* violence or suicide or permanent estrangement. Not in Colwin Land. (I'm not sure punk ever happened in Colwin Land, either.) Her people are blithe and clueless about some things, like money and class. But they are also earnest and lovable, and such wrecks in their way, bumbling around Manhattan into friendships and marriages and extramarital entanglements and amorphous variations on all three. In Colwin Land, people tend to marry someone they've known since age five and then wander into love affairs that play themselves out and end on a wistful note, all without ruining anyone's life.

I discovered Laurie Colwin at age sixteen, in my heavily lacquered Florida hometown where people wanted you to know *exactly* how much money they had and showed it off by wearing lots of gold and driving big white cars with white leather seats. My friends' fathers wore Italian loafers and had deep golfers' tans. My father was a tenured professor, which in a lot of towns would have counted as a prestigious and well-paying gig but in Boca Raton made us seem sort of poor. My sister and I had ballet classes and orthodontic work and hand-me-down cars and all the other middle-class accoutrements of American youth, but compared with the yachts and Gucci bags of my classmates, we looked kind of janky. Colwin Land is also a rich-person playground, of course, but one where being an academic and wearing the same shoes for years in a row is cool. And in Colwin Land, men fall hopelessly in love with women based on how they look while reading a newspaper, or the fact that they have odd skills such as wildflower identification or lamp repair. At sixteen I sometimes felt as if I had nothing *but* oddities to offer the opposite sex. Reading Colwin gave me a vision of the future where someone might love me for at least one of them.

What seemed newest of all about Laurie Colwin back

then, and still feels radical now, was her obsession with the pursuit of happiness. Ensconced in their comfortable lives, her characters have the time and psychic space to think about it—what it means, and how to get it. When I found her, I was up to my ears in the neon nihilism of Bret Easton Ellis and Jay McInerney. I was tired of misery, at least in books. (I was tired of my own misery, too, but I also knew there wasn't a lot a teenager stuck at the wrong school in the wrong town in the wrong state could do about that, so I bided my time and tried to play off depression as glamour.) I respected Colwin for taking happiness seriously, which I thought was probably harder than giving your characters cocaine nosebleeds.

As I grew out of my parents' home and into the world, had boyfriends and apartments and travels, her novels became a constant in my life, both as a comfort and as an aesthetic: the sense that tight-stretched sheets and a perfectly roasted chicken were things worth caring about, because they alchemized into something like happiness. When I was lonely and snowed in at graduate school, I read about the solitude-loving Holly Sturgis in *Happy All the Time* and thought how she would have relished the thick quiet of a blizzard and the impossibility of leaving home. When a boy situation ended badly and I was sure I'd never fall in love again, I would reread *Shine On, Bright and Dangerous Object* and realize that if its twenty-seven-year-old widow heroine could rebound with her own brother-in-law, surely I could find someone to replace whatever sad-sack indie-rock guy had broken my heart. Colwin taught me to pay attention to the everyday things around me. I bought anemones for my kitchen table and a Wedgwood saucer for my house keys and an oval platter for my perfectly roasted chickens. And sure enough, over time these details added up to, if not happiness, at least the sense that I could quietly define my own life and taste based on small domestic pleasures.

By the time of my trip to Paris, I was almost forty and still reread my favorite Colwin books often, but they had started to make me sad. Like her people, I now lived in a big city and had witty and urbane friends. I had no trust fund to relax into, but I'd made enough money on my own to surround myself with beautiful art and clothes and food. But I also lived in a constant state of low-level panic over work and the creeping sense that my time on earth was flying by and I had no lasting accomplishments or even passions to show for it. To soothe that panic, I drank wine, a lot of it. Colwin's characters certainly know their way around a glass of cold, dry white wine, and when I'd first started drinking regularly, I felt like one of them, having wide-ranging conversations with friends at sidewalk cafés. But once I'd worked up to a bottle a night in my living room, alone, I could no longer pretend the sparkling people of Colwin Land and I had much in common, and reading about them felt like a way to punish myself for slipping so far.

I left the Village Voice and wandered down to a café where I had coffee and a ham tartine. I congratulated myself for not ordering wine. The congratulations were dubiously earned, because I didn't actually enjoy daylight drinking and hardly ever did it. One day drink just made me groggy. Two made me feel good, but then I had to keep topping up the tank or risk the dreaded 3:00 p.m. come-down: too sober for euphoria, too tipsy to get anything done. The only help for it was to keep drinking into the night, and even at my worst I wasn't in the habit of doing that. Still, at this point I was looking for any opportunity to praise myself for drinking behavior that normal people would take for granted. If that meant giving myself brownie points for not doing something I didn't want to do, so be it.

I read the first chapter of *Happy All the Time*, in which the muddled romantics Vincent and Guido are trying to escape the Cambridge summer heat and "found them-selves perusing an exhibition of Greek vases at the Fogg Museum." *What would it be like to be a person who just* found herself *in museums or who had opinions about vases?* I won-dered. What would it be like to be a person who knew her third cousins, or spent time with *any* of her relatives? I was so wrapped up both in the novel and in comparing myself negatively to it that some time passed before I noticed that Rue Princesse had become still and quiet, with occasional bursts of frantic male sounds. I looked around for the source of the noise and saw the backs of maybe thirty men crammed into the open-air bar across the street, staring at two big televisions. Many of them had on soccer scarves or were festooned with bits of red streamers, the kind that fly out of Roman candles. The men would stare intently at the match and then yell en masse at the TVs. I tried to remem-ber the last time I had yelled in public. It didn't seem like the kind of thing I would do, but then, neither did hating Paris. Though I wasn't sure I hated Paris quite so much anymore.

The walk back to the Saint-Germain Metro stop was similar: silence/yelling/silence/yelling. The platform was unusually empty for a Saturday, and the train car, too. I had no destination in mind; I only knew I wasn't ready to return to my hotel, which looked like a long-abandoned *Dynasty* set, with employees wandering around the lobby in elaborate tasseled uniforms that had possibly not been cleaned in years. So, for several stops I sat and read about the morning following Guido's first night with his beloved, the cool and unflappable Holly. He sits at her kitchen table, dazzled and panicked—*flapped*—watching her read the newspaper as though it were any other day.

Poor Guido is fucked. Of course, I knew that Holly is just trying to maintain a facade of normality because strong feelings terrify her. But my sympathies lay mainly with him, maybe because while I'd long wanted to be a serene Holly, I was in fact a total Guido. I was contemplating this when the doors opened at Saint-Michel and ten preteen boys in matching soccer scarves burst onto the train singing a fight song. If they had been a few years older, their rowdiness might have been annoying or even unnerving. But they were still children, and they delighted and mystified me. Where had they come from? What would it be like to be someone who sang in public? To be a boy in a boy pack, owning the subway? I didn't feel that free in my own car.

I followed the boys off the train at Châtelet and changed lines for the Tuileries. Yes, historically, the Tuileries had caused me to feel old and unsexy. But I knew I could buy ice cream there. And anyway, the word "tuileries" was one thing I had always unequivocally loved about Paris. As I approached the steps to the surface, the usual urine smell blended and was overtaken by something sweet. Specifically sweet. I put a name to it just before I reached street level and saw the pink and blue cotton-candy blobs, and then the carousel and Tilt-A-Whirl and ringtoss booth and chestnut cart.

Grieving and unsettled, Kristi Coulter had spent the afternoon reading in Saint-Germain and now found herself at a carnival in the Tuileries. I smiled for the first time in days and then waded in.

This is why I drank, you know. Because I wanted every day to be like that. I wanted every day to feel like a movie montage, or at least to end in an epiphany, or at least to have a clear narrative arc, or at least to make some level of sense. I thought that if I engineered my highs and lows, I could become one of Laurie Colwin's lovable bumblers: a bit dotty, sure, but also decent, thoughtful, and wiser than they know. I didn't see that I already was one. I couldn't see it because, also in Colwin fashion, I was a little clueless about myself. And because somewhere along the way I'd forgotten that just because her people are smart, sophisticated, and surrounded by beautiful things, that doesn't make them happy. They're pursuing happiness. By using wine to engineer my life, I was pursuing happiness, too. Just not in a way that was ever going to work.

Four years later I will be sober and sitting at a scratched café table in my tree-lined neighborhood, the Seattle version of Colwin Land, and I will be in a muddle like you wouldn't believe: about how I should earn a living, about a married man my married self might be falling in love with, about whether I'll ever be at peace with how these dark, wet winters dampen my mood. Where's my daily epiphany? Where is the random sign that will tell me if my aim is true? Where's the *sense*?

None of those things will be available—not that day, not on call, no matter how much I want them. And I really do. I want to find the perfectly absorbing job, to accept all weather with stolid good cheer, to have a kitchen full of copper pots and blue roses. I want happiness. But moping in that Seattle café, I will know that at least I'm *pursuing* happiness in a way that works. Mostly. And I will have figured out that sometimes pursuit just means paying close attention to the story while it emerges in its own damn time.

I didn't know any of this that day in the Tuileries, but at the time a carnival was enough. I rode the Tilt-A-Whirl and bought some cotton candy that caught the late-afternoon light just so. Someone's dog nosed me in the crotch, and I laughed and told his mortified owner it was no problem and kissed him on the head, just to kiss in the Tuileries. The next morning, I woke with a wine headache and a sense that I'd still lost something forever. I sat up in bed for a minute, and then I walked to the window and looked at the Paris skyline.

Pretty, I thought.

Deadlifting

"Is life about coming to terms with not living out our childhood dreams?"

All Seattleites get like this by March, our fifth straight
sunless month. *Has my career peaked already? Does anyone
really love me? Can my body still process vitamin D?* And Noah,
despite growing up in a similarly gloomy European climate, is no exception. We are slumped in side-by-side red
armchairs, staring out the coffee shop window at a cop
ticketing parked cars, and he wants to know why life feels
less boldly colored than his kid self had planned. "It's not
all dashed hopes," I say. "Have I told you about the time
I was a clown in the circus?"

There was this Ringling Brothers essay contest: "Why
I Want to Be a Circus Clown." I told my mother exactly
what to write: "When I grow up, I want to be a surgeon at
night and a clown in the daytime so I will never have to go
to bed and go to sleep. I have thought about this for years."
I was five.

I won the contest and spent a full day as a grease-painted

circus professional. Clowning was underwhelming, to be honest. I had no interest in it, despite what I claimed (though it was true that I planned to become a surgeon, for reasons that escape me now). I just wanted to win. And mostly, I wanted to write.

"Obviously, I didn't become a surgeon," I say to Noah. "And I didn't join the circus, though sometimes it feels like I did." He laughs. We're co-workers on a secret project whose direction, schedule, and personnel shift dramatically every few months. Half of my closest teammates have quit or been fired since I joined the team a year ago, because, as we now know, clowning is not for everyone. "But I am a writer."

"So your circus dream came true," Noah says.

"Yeah. I guess so. Maybe you're living out a childhood vision, too, and you just don't know it." What I'm thinking, but don't yet know how to say out loud, is *Does anyone know what they're becoming until they've become it?* I'd been running for three years before I realized I was a runner. I'd been drinking for twenty-five before I knew I was a drunk.

I was riding in a friend's car just outside Ann Arbor in my early twenties when an old Jackson Browne song came on the radio. "This is you," my friend said, throwing me a sidelong glance. I listened for a few minutes and then squinted at him. "Am I the fountain of sorrow, or light? Don't tell me, I think I know." He was a prickly man, not big on compliments. And also I spent a lot of time crying in his presence, over work or just quarter-life angst. He never tried to make me stop, just waited serenely until I did.

"Correct," he said, with his half smile.

"I could be a fucking fountain of light if I wanted to be," I told him, feet on the dashboard.

"There's hope for you yet," he said.

Many years later I understood he'd been trying to say he loved me. I know this because he texted me the song in the middle of the night with the words "I WAS TRYING TO SAY I LOVED YOU." But I'm not one to rub drunk texts in people's faces, so I never did tell him that he'd been right. There *had* been hope for me after all.

The day after I talk to Noah, I run ten miles. I'd rather not, but the training plan says to do it, and I have long since learned the value of listening to experts. Without distraction, a piercing loneliness can overtake me by mile six of a long run, especially when the weather is this wet and windy. To stave that off, I listen to a podcast featuring two women with decades of sobriety between them. The topic is willpower. "I have none of it. *None,*" one of the women says, laughing. "But people congratulate me on it, just because I'm sober. They think I've been using willpower for twenty years."

I smile in recognition because people say those things to me, too: "You're so *strong.* You're so *focused.*" I deadlift a 140-pound barbell ten times a week; *that* makes me feel strong and focused. Otherwise, it's more like dreamy and easily distracted. I once dropped everything to research duck anatomy because someone mentioned on Facebook that there's nothing weirder in nature than a duck's penis. That led to browsing on Nordstrom.com because that's what happens almost any time I drop down the rabbit hole, which probably led to a denim purchase and shoes, and so on. This is not the behavior of someone who has exceptional strength and focus, someone you could imagine using her mental powers to, say, make cars fly through the air, or refreeze the polar ice caps, or keep herself from drinking a bottle of Marsanne each day.

It starts to rain as I run another half mile through Montlake, but I'm busy thinking about how silly people are to assume not drinking is *so hard*. It doesn't take willpower to avoid the thing that is sure to ruin my life; it just takes a fierce, overriding desire to not ruin my life. In the light of that desire, the necessary behaviors and habits don't seem like such a big deal. But God knows I didn't always see it that way. When I first quit, I was sure the rest of my life would be like deadlifting. I'd been working with a trainer for a year, and he had me focused on building up my core strength, which meant lifting a heavy weight off the ground slowly, with no help from momentum. Deadlifting requires strength, focus, and ferocity. There's the deep squat before the weights are even in hand. The moment that the weight comes off the ground and becomes your problem. The tightening in your hips and lats because picking up a hundred and forty pounds requires the sides of your body to suck inward and create a column of power. And then, once you've survived the slow drag up to standing, the slower, scarier trip back down, using every tiny shoulder muscle to keep your arms in their sockets, and sitting so deep in your hips that you almost fall over backward, before finally setting the bar down. And then doing it all again. And again. I thought living booze-free would feel just like that, and the prize would be the satisfaction of knowing I could work that hard all day, every day, and survive.

Running up a long hill—seems like all Seattle hills are long ones—makes me feel trapped, and feeling trapped makes me angry. When I get to the top, I put my hands on my knees and gasp for breath, and that's when the past rushes over me in dark waves. Standing still with my eyes closed, waiting out the urge to pour a drink. Twitching at the phantom-limb sensation of a wineglass stem in my hand. Pretending to listen to a friend when all I could hear in my head was *I don't drink anymore.* That first dinner party, plane ride, vacation, fight, Christmas, without anything to make it easier. The shattering tenderness I suddenly felt for the street drunks in Pioneer Square. Those early months *were* like deadlifting, and what I was hauling up wasn't just my wine habit but my whole lumpy life. Two lives, really. One belonged to an exhausted, angry, overworked woman who regarded herself with skepticism, at best. The other belonged to the same woman, but newly stripped of the bottle that made the rest tolerable.

"Don't think of the barbell as a separate thing," my weight trainer told me once, when I was struggling to lift it. "Just pretend it's part of your arms, and stand up." At some point my addiction and what came after had become like that barbell: just a part of my body. I didn't have to pick them up and tote them around, because I'd made space for them to live within me.

The dogs greet me in the entry hall with their usual *roo-roo-roos*. John hears the noise from his third-floor office—it can likely be heard from space—and comes downstairs to say hi. "I realized something!" I say when I hear him on the stairs. "I'm a sober person."

"Yes," he says as he makes his way to me, "for several years now."

"I know, but I forgot. I thought I was just a regular kind of person. But I'm not! I quit drinking."

John makes it to the lower landing and cocks his head at me. "So, uh, how's everything going there?"

I'm standing stark naked in a ring of sodden clothes, shivering and mascara streaked, wringing out my hair onto the flagstone tiles of our entry hall. The dogs have each claimed one of my wet socks and are lying by the Christmas cactus, slurping them. My nails are blue—only a little, but even a little is less than ideal.

"It rained," I say.

"It was a *monsoon*. I texted you to see if you needed a rescue."

I check my phone. So he did. The rain had started to seem maliciously aggressive in the last few miles, but it had never occurred to me to stop. We live in water here.

"You're shaking," John says. He gets a towel from the laundry room and holds it out to me.

"I'm shaking with accumulated change," I say.

"Okay, but take the towel anyway." And I do. Just because your heart is quaking is no reason not to dry your hair.

"So much has happened since I quit," I say. "I don't know how anyone *changes* this much. In retrospect it's exhausting."

"Or maybe you're exhausted because you just ran ten miles in a storm like a lunatic," John says.

"Yeah," I say vaguely, but those wet, tough miles already feel far behind me, just as those early sober days did until an hour ago and probably will again soon enough. I'm too woozy to explain that to John right now. Instead, I march my naked body and turbaned head up the stairs to take a hot shower. But on the way I see the bed, and then I'm tucked in it. All the jagged parts of me fall asleep in moments, and when I wake, it's still light out and the wind is still howling but I smell coffee downstairs.

For months after I quit drinking, my first waking thought was often still *How hungover am I today?* Sometimes, like now, I still wake up that way. *How hungover am I? How hard will I have to work to hide it?* I tense for the answer, and then I remember. I'm not hungover. There's nothing to hide. And I'm only one woman now. My muscles unclench and I lie in bed being her.

Acknowledgments

Two years ago, Daphne Durham read "Girl Skulks into a Room" and saw a book in it. I thought that was crazy talk, and now here I am publicly admitting I was wrong. Daphne, thank you for your persuasion, for your phenomenal eye and ear, and for always knowing when to push me a little further and when to pull me back from the ledge. In addition to making my No. 1 childhood dream come true, you made this book better in every way. I can't imagine having had a better partner, and that all this comes on top of a decade of friendship is nearly enough to turn me into an optimist.

Thank you also to everyone at MCD/FSG who helped bring this thing into the world: Sean McDonald, Sara Birmingham, Alex Merto, Sarita Varma, Katie Hurley, Naomi Huffman, Jackson Howard, Debra Helfand, Nina Frieman, and Jonathan Lippincott. Thank you to Sarah Burnes of the Gernert Company; I'm so glad we found each other. Thank you to Silvia Killingsworth of *The Awl* for giving me a space to develop some of the pieces in this book, and to

Steph Georgopulos at *Medium* for being Tweeter Zero of the Enjoli Virus. "I think you might be changing my life," I told her that day, and it turned out to be true.

Thank you to everyone who provided some combination of companionship, coffee, feedback, love, and healthy distraction along the way, especially Chris Aguirre, Hilary Bailey Burnett, Claire Dederer, Claire Rudy Foster, Mary Ellen Fullhart, David Gellman, the HOME girls, Jason Kirk, Thomas Mathiesen, Laura McKowen, Richelle Ricard, Holly Glenn Whitaker, and Chris Woodstra. Thank you to Mindy Oliver, the most true-blue human being in the world. Thank you to my co-workers for embracing both the worker and the writer sides of me, and especially to Aaron Nather and Gianna Puerini, who didn't bat an eye when I said, "Hey, I need to take four months off to finish this thing." Thank you to Richard Holt for reading me exactly the right poem in act 1. Thank you to Sandra Coffman for reminding me that reality and my lunatic thoughts are not always one and the same. Thank you to my parents for teaching me to read at age two. I love you.

Thank you to Belle Robertson for making the idea of a day without a drink seem not only plausible but appealing. Thank you to everyone I've ever met who has heard me say, "No thanks, I don't drink," without responding, "Really? Why not?"

Most of all, thank you to John Sindelar, my Big Love, my legal boyfriend. And to Linus and Ella: the most shoe-box-headed, Frito-footed, blissfully addled dogs on earth, whom I love in exactly equal amounts.